BRIGHT NOTES

THE RED PONY AND THE PEARL BY JOHN STEINBECK

Intelligent Education

Nashville, Tennessee

BRIGHT NOTES: The Red Pony and The Pearl
www.BrightNotes.com

No part of this publication may be used or reproduced in any manner whatsoever without written permission, except in the case of brief quotations in critical articles and reviews. For permissions, contact Influence Publishers http://www.influencepublishers.com.

ISBN: 978-1-645422-82-2 (Paperback)
ISBN: 978-1-645422-83-9 (eBook)

Published in accordance with the U.S. Copyright Office Orphan Works and Mass Digitization report of the register of copyrights, June 2015.

Originally published by Monarch Press.
Armand Schwerner, 1965
2020 Edition published by Influence Publishers.

Interior design by Lapiz Digital Services. Cover Design by Thinkpen Designs.

Printed in the United States of America.

Library of Congress Cataloging-in-Publication Data forthcoming.
Names: Intelligent Education
Title: BRIGHT NOTES: The Red Pony and The Pearl
Subject: STU004000 STUDY AIDS / Book Notes

CONTENTS

1) Introduction to John Steinbeck	1
2) The Red Pony: Textual Analysis	
Parts I and II	14
Parts III and IV	29
3) The Red Pony: Character Analyses	40
4) The Pearl: Textual Analysis	
Chapters I–III	46
Chapters IV–VI	65
5) The Pearl: Character Analyses	79
6) Critical Commentary	84
7) Essay Questions and Answers	89
8) Bibliography	94

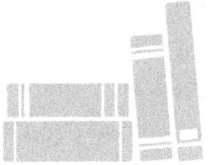

INTRODUCTION TO JOHN STEINBECK

EARLY DAYS

John Steinbeck's father, who came to California shortly after the Civil War, for many years occupied a position as treasurer of Monterey County; the novelist's mother was a teacher in the public schools of the Salinas Valley. In contrast with the farther-ranging locales found in the fictions of Hemingway and Henry James, the frequent appearance in Steinbeck's novels and stories of the California valleys and their inhabitants underlines the novelist's link with his parents' involvements. John Ernst Steinbeck, born in Salinas on February 27, 1902, repeatedly demonstrates in his work his sensitivity to nature and to natural processes, so much of which he studied and learned about in the context of the California where he was born and which he loved. His fiction abounds with the *paisanos*, the migrant laborers, the exploited men and women, the union organizers, and the marine scientists whose affections, concerns and fears the writer had such abundant opportunity to observe. What is more, Steinbeck has made statements about his early years testifying to his experience of literature at home—he mentions *Paradise Lost, Crime and Punishment, The Return of the Native*, and *Madame Bovary* among others as works with which he had a very early acquaintance. Here, no doubt, his mother's profession contributed directly to the burgeoning writer's direction. Nor was his father uninvolved in the boy's artistic adventures; Steinbeck's early fiction was written in cast-off accountant's ledgers!

FROM HIGH SCHOOL TO THE FIRST NOVEL

Steinbeck kept very busy in high school. He wrote for the school paper; he belonged to the basketball and track teams; he was elected president of his senior class. When school was out, he spent vacations working as a hired hand on local ranches. After he graduated, and before his entrance to Stanford University, he worked as an assistant chemist in a local sugar-beet factory. His attendance at Stanford was not continuous. He was an English major, attended intermittently over a period of five years, but did not get a degree; he wrote some vagabond stories and poems, commonly satirical, for the college newspaper and magazine. Perhaps as important to his future career as his academic involvement were his periods of employment while he was not attending classes. He worked on ranches and on a road gang, where he learned about verbal and behavioral traits which he later incorporated into his work. In later years he would write to his agents letters justifying unusual aspects of conversational passages in his books by drawing on his memory of such observations. In 1925, having amassed less than half the number of credits required for graduation, Steinbeck left Stanford permanently; he went to New York City to become a writer. His brief stay, unsuccessful and anonymous, interestingly recalls William Faulkner's journey to New York five years before. Of all major 20th century American novelists probably these two made the most consistent and profound use of their provincial environment; both disliked large urban centers. Faulkner too had come to the big city right after brief stays at the local university—the University of Mississippi. Where Steinbeck worked for a brief and unsatisfactory while as a reporter on the New York *American*, Faulkner spent a similarly short and equally unpleasant time in the book department of Lord and Taylor's department store. And like Steinbeck, Faulkner left New York quickly and went back to his home area; Steinbeck failed in his attempt to publish some short stories in New York and returned home as a deck hand on a ship that crossed the Panama Canal. When he returned to New York City fifteen years later as a famous writer, he still viewed the city unfavorably. In California again, Steinbeck got a job as caretaker of a Lake Tahoe estate; he was fired from that position when a tree fell through the roof. He then worked in a fish hatchery nearby. During this period, amounting to approximately two years, the writer finished his first novel to be published, *Cup of God, A Life of Sir Henry Morgan, Buccaneer, with Occasional Reference to History.* It was his fourth attempt at a novel, got few reviews and little recognition.

THE SALINAS VALLEY

This valley, "Steinbeck country," runs roughly north and south, paralleling the California coast about thirty miles from the shoreline. The southern end of the valley, divided into large fields, grows lettuce, broccoli and other vegetables; cattle feed on nearby hill slopes. The town of Salinas itself, Steinbeck's home town, ten miles from Monterey Bay, is the county seat—somewhat urbanized, but essentially involved with the growers, cattlemen and workers of the area. The lettuce-growing complex has been the scene of severe labor-management disputes; before the second World War a strike by the local workers was ruthlessly put down. During this period normal judicial processes were suspended, violence characterized some aspects of the struggle, and after a month the union lost. The region in general features interestingly divergent social groups. The picturesque harbor includes fishermen and cannery workers from various backgrounds, Japanese, Portuguese and Italian, involved largely with the sardine trade. In addition, survivals from old Spanish mission days draw interested tourists. Carmel is not far; artists and writers have found it a congenial home and find its lack of rigid social rules inviting.

A TERRAIN OF EXTREMES

Carey McWilliams has underlined idiosyncratic aspects of the vineyards, orchards and ranches in the area. While the old tradition of individual' initiative and adventure still remains, as embodied in the lifestyles of fishermen, aspects of bohemian socialization and some traits of ranch hand behavior, vegetable growing and cattle raising are highly collectivized. These industries are big business and feature a distinct separation between ownership and management. Freeman Champney points out that the region has been typically a terrain of extremes—poverty and riches, economic upper class and mobile, untutored working people. The area lacked a stable middle class, and all the continuous, responsible communal concern that such a class often has. The reader will note the relevance of these sociological observations when he examines *Of Mice and Men*. Another environmental feature of the greatest importance to the development of Steinbeck's thinking is the proliferation of marine life in the Bay. With Edward Ricketts, a marine biologist and close friend, Steinbeck in 1941 published *Sea of Cortez*, a journal of travel and research in marine biology. This study summed up some aspects of the novelist's long-standing interest in animal behavior and scientific objectivity. Its particular relevance will be discussed in the Critical Commentary.

THE SECOND NOVEL

In 1930, at the age of twenty-eight, Steinbeck married. He went to live in Pacific Grove; his father gave him $25.00 a month and a small house. He wrote 30,000 words of a novel, and a thriller, *Murder at Full Moon*. The latter, a piece of hack work done in the hope of earning some quick cash, he was unhappy with. He withdrew both from his agents. His next important work, published in 1933, was *To a God Unknown*, a novel in which Steinbeck suggests the deep-lying need of man for ritualistic and magical behavior. Neither of the first two published novels made money but Steinbeck kept on; he was also writing short stories, planning some articles based on a tentative 400-mile horseback trip in Mexico, and working intermittently on odd jobs. The first of his stories to be printed were the first two parts of *The Red Pony*, in the *North American Review* of November and December 1933. The trip to Mexico was cancelled because of the pressure of writing, and Steinbeck worked at odd jobs until 1936-1937.

PAISANOS AND PROPERTY; THE THIRD NOVEL

Steinbeck's third novel found an appreciative audience and made money. *Tortilla Flat* was published in 1935, received an award, was produced as a play and was sold to the movies. Consistent to his pattern, Steinbeck in this book drew upon incidents he had observed—in this case episodes stemming from the lives of workers in the sugar-beet factory where he had worked years before. In the life of his *paisanos*, described in a mock-epic style, the novelist emphasizes values subtly critical of middle-class morality. The characters lie, forgivably, steal, forgivably, and continually rationalize, forgivably; these traits, commonly defined as unworthy in a middle-class context, are not presented as heinous in the culture depicted. Steinbeck does not so much support his characters' attitudes, poor diets and uncleanliness as he deplores the larger society's consuming and corrupting concern with *property* and the inimical values derived from owning property. Steinbeck suggests that the loyalty and spontaneity characteristics *within* his subcultural group cannot exist within the middle class American culture. Consistent with a good deal of later criticism of Steinbeck's work, Edmund Wilson, the influential critic, stated that the *paisanos* were such rudimentary creatures that they existed nearly on an animal level. Such statements, referring also to *Of Mice and Men*, can be neither easily refuted nor easily supported. For some critics, Steinbeck is a maudlin sentimentalist; for others he writes as a compassionate and tragic novelist.

IN DUBIOUS BATTLE

In 1936, Steinbeck published the strike novel, *In Dubious Battle*, which received critical praise, and is written in an objective, detached prose. Accusations of sentimentality find little direct support in this novel, for while the workers are depicted clearly as victims of others' machinations, the laborers themselves are no saints untouched by violence and meanness. Perhaps the most interesting philosophical aspect of *In Dubious Battle* involves the role played by an important character, Doc Burton, whose ideas are closely paralleled in Steinbeck's later work, *Sea of Cortez*, mentioned previously. In that 1941 book the novelist refers to his theory of "group-man," a concept very important to Steinbeck, who attributes to human groups an identity qualitatively different from the mere sum of contributing individual behavior traits. The novelist develops his theory on the basis of an analogy with the observed behavior of marine invertebrates, which seem to operate as a body for the gratification of certain primitive needs.

THE RED PONY

We have noted that the *North American Review* published two stories which were to become the first two parts of *The Red Pony*. In 1937, four years later, and one year after the publication of *In Dubious Battle*, Covici-Friede published a deluxe edition of *The Red Pony*, which included only 699 copies, each numbered and signed by the author. This first edition contains three sections: "The Gift," "The Great Mountains," and "The Promise." The following year Viking Press put out *The Long Valley*, a collection of stories. *The Red Pony* was reprinted in this anthology of Steinbeck's short fiction, but this time it amounted to four parts, including now "The Leader of the People," previously unpublished anywhere. (The three sections which made up the original Covici-Friede edition *had* all appeared before that 1937 publication. For details of first appearance see *Bibliography*.) In 1945 Viking published *The Red Pony* in an illustrated edition which again contained all four sections. This long story, or novella, is the story of a young boy's development, his confrontations with violence, loss, and death, written in a prose which recaptures the magical tone of childhood. The fourth section, "Leader of the People," is not as essentially a part of the novella as the first three, but does find its place in the whole as a kind of philosophical afterword in the form of a narrative. The homogeneity of the entire four-part version is greatly enhanced by the particular quality of the style, which allies a realistic tone with a lyrically poetic direction.

OF MICE AND MEN

This novel deals with ranch workers, two of whom are singled out for particular consideration. Lennie, huge, powerful and moronic, depends utterly on his comrade and guide George for protection and warmth. This novel, Steinbeck's first immediate and nationwide success, nearly did not see the light of a publishing day. The novelist's setter pup ate up about half of the manuscript, and no other draft existed. Steinbeck humorously suggested the poor dog might have been acting critically and merely gave the pup an ordinary spanking. It took months to rewrite the munched material. The Book-of-the-Month Club selected the novel in the year of publication, 1937; *Of Mice and Men* appeared on the best-seller lists; it was sold to Hollywood, where one producer absurdly suggested to the author that someone else commit the murder for which Lennie is responsible in the novel—in order to preserve the audience's sympathy for the poor brute! Finally independent, Steinbeck traveled to New York where he saw his agent, attended a dinner for Thomas Mann in a borrowed suit and sailed to England, after which he visited the home of his mother's people in Ireland. He then went on to Sweden and Russia.

THE NOVEL BECOMES A PLAY

When he returned to the United States, Steinbeck stayed at a Bucks County, Pennsylvania farm belonging to George Kaufman, the famous musical comedy librettist; there, with some useful suggestions by Kaufman (who was to direct the play) the acting version was finished. It opened on November 23, 1937 at the Music Box Theatre in New York City, to great applause. It elicited very favorable critical response, so much so that the play won the Drama Critics' Circle Award in a season which also featured such important plays as *Our Town* and *Golden Boy*. The citation awarded the play said:

> The New York Drama Critics' Circle awards its prize to John Steinbeck's *Of Mice and Men* for its direct force

and perception in handling a theme genuinely rooted in American life; for its bite into the strict quality of its material; for his refusal to make this study of tragical loneliness and frustration either cheap or sensational; and finally for its simple, intense and steadily rising effect on the stage.

THE GRAPES OF WRATH

Steinbeck had not waited to see the play produced. As soon as he finished writing the stage version he set out for Oklahoma, where he joined a group of migrant workers. He lived with them in their shanties, and accompanied them to California, working all the way. He stated several times during this period that he had no preconceived theories, social or economic, with which to confront the exploitation and forced mobility typical of the migrant laborers. He was with them to see, to hear, and to experience. He hoped that the projection of his individual adventure onto a larger social pattern would be meaningful. Steinbeck's intense compassion for the poverty and misery of his co-workers did not lead to either sentimentalism or inappropriately "objective" stylization. However, the novel penetrated America's consciousness like a bomb, and that explosion left relatively little room for sober critical appraisal. The book was reviled; it was-celebrated; it was damned for its inaccuracies, for giving an unfair and distorted picture of the United States to the world; it was scolded for not being a sufficiently stringent picture of deprivation, illness and victimization. It was read; it was seen as a movie; it was debated on the radio. In short the novel had isolated a sore and vulnerable part of the American conscience. The coming of war to Europe at this time, 1939, merely increased Steinbeck's despairing sense that the short period of human civilizations had had no perceptible effect on the animalistic violences implicit in man's oldest impulses.

SEA OF CORTEZ

In March of 1949 Steinbeck, in the company of his marine biologist friend, Edward Ricketts, traveled to the Gulf of California with the purpose of studying and classifying a number of marine invertebrates in the Gulf—also known as the Sea of Cortez, the old name and one which Steinbeck used as the title of the book. The importance of this work has been suggested before. In it, Steinbeck, the author of one of the two journals reproduced in *Sea of Cortez*, emphasizes the importance of a concept which he called "non-teleological thought." This term involves Steinbeck's attitude toward reality, which he feels should not be understood so much as a result of certain causal principles as it should be experienced in the immediate present, without an overlay of analytical considerations. Such considerations help to explain Steinbeck's obvious fondness for a whole series of fictive characters for whom dancing, singing and drinking *now* are more important and gratifying than grinding concern for tomorrow. The speculations in *Sea of Cortez*, however, lead to serious problems for Steinbeck's reader, who often can note puzzling discrepancies in both the structure and the depth of character portrayals in Steinbeck's works.

STEINBECK AND WORLD WAR II

The American involvement in World War II took place in the very month that *Sea of Cortez* was published. Steinbeck did what he could for the war effort. With Ricketts, he put together a list of scientific papers written by Japanese zoologists; these papers supplied information about tides and related matters which the novelist thought would be useful to the United States in the event of an invasion of the Japanese islands. Apparently these submissions were not acted upon. Peter Lisca, a critic who has most extensively written about Steinbeck, states that in addition to this effort, Steinbeck suggested that counterfeit money be dropped behind enemy lines in order to cause inflation; it seems that President Roosevelt actually approved of this scheme, which was subsequently rejected by the Secretary of the Treasury. Steinbeck then wrote *Bombs Away*, a report about the Air Force's men and equipment; the novelist flew to a number of bases, accompanied by a photographer, in order to learn first-hand about the subject under investigation. In 1943 Steinbeck began a series of communiques from Europe and Africa for the New York *Herald Tribune.* These pieces dealt generally with individuals in the service, and their emotions, rather than with military analysis. During this period Steinbeck also published a novel of the Nazi occupation of Norway, *The Moon is Down*, which created vast excitement and drew both passionate apologists and angry accusations. The latter strongly underlined their opinions that Steinbeck's portrayal of the Nazi occupiers of Norway insisted too much on their common humanity and glimpsed too little of their fundamental evil. Although the King of Norway decorated Steinbeck for the book, present critics, now somewhat outside the heat of the war context, can identify the relative shallowness of the character portrayals, and the lack of creative tensions in the novel.

CANNERY ROW

In December 1944, *Cannery Row* was published. A novel about individuals who in a middle-class situation would be seen as misfits and irresponsibles, it appears to praise even more positively than *Tortilla Flat* the hedonistic virtues exempt from the usual social-climbing gastric ulcered vaults of ambition. In addition, the novel features Doc, a character interestingly similar to Ed Ricketts, in whom are allied the virtues of the biological scientist's essential affectionate detachment and the common touch. In fact, the resemblance between the character and Ricketts was so clear that *Life* magazine wanted to do a feature on the marine biologist; although he rejected this invasion of his privacy, he and his laboratory nevertheless became a center of interest.

THE PEARL

In December of 1945 *Woman's Home Companion* printed a story called "The Pearl of the World," reprinted by Viking Press in 1947 as *The Pearl*. It is the story of a young man in Bolivia, who with his wife and little infant boy lives in primitive conditions. His discovery of an immensely valuable pearl triggers dishonesty and rapacity among the pearl brokers, dissension in his own family, and eventually brings death to the little boy. The Viking edition came out in December, 1947, to coincide with the premiere of the movie version, for which Steinbeck himself had written the adaptation. The basic story had been in the novelist's mind for at least four years; he relates the tale as he first heard of it in *Sea of Cortez*, but the later version entails the introduction of several new characters and some alteration of the story line for the purposes of dramatic verisimilitude.

SOME LATER WORK; THE NOBEL PRIZE

Steinbeck wrote a number of novels after *The Pearl*, including *The Wayward Bus* and *East of Eden*, and in the sixties, *Travels with Charley* and *The Winter of our Discontent.* The *Travels* sold extremely well; it is a journal kept by the novelist of his visits to some forty states with a companionable dog. Most of the "travels" take place outside the great urban centers of the United States, thus avoiding the almost overwhelming problems raised by the extraordinary growth and complexity of 20th century metropolitan reality. Although the novelist's domestic critical reputation was generally on the downgrade from the period of the second World War to the present, and although his later work often departs from the themes he addressed powerfully in the thirties, the Nobel Prize Committee awarded him the Prize for 1962. He had published *The Winter of our Discontent* the year before, but the general critical and journalistic consensus was that the Nobel Prize had been awarded to Steinbeck primarily in belated recognition of such novels as *The Grapes of Wrath*, published many years before. The citation reads in part:

> Among the masters of modern American literature who have already been awarded this prize ... Steinbeck more than holds his own, independent in position and achievement... His sympathies always go out to the oppressed, the misfits and the distressed.

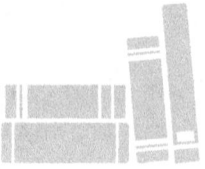

THE RED PONY

TEXTUAL ANALYSIS

PARTS I AND II

PART I: THE GIFT

Synopsis

Billy Buck is the only ranchhand working at the Tiflin ranch. He appears initially in this first section (one of four). When the triangle rings the breakfast signal, he, the senior Tiflin-Carl and ten-year-old Jody come in to the table. Mrs. Tiflin prepares the food; she never sits down with the men and boy. After breakfast Jody goes to his favorite nook near the ranchhouse from where he can see the main house and the bunkhouse where Billy lives. The nook holds a wooden tub that catches the spring water carried by a pipe. Around the tub there is always a deep green grassy area, no matter what the weather: the spot symbolizes sanity and health throughout the novella. After the boy comes back from school he usually does chores-gathering eggs and firewood. This particular evening Carl and Billy Buck have brandy on their breaths, a common sign that some good stories are promised. But there are none; the boy goes to sleep and hears his father chuckle.

The next morning the father harshly orders the boy to come along to the barn. (Billy's absolute obedience is stressed in the narrative.) Jody is overwhelmed; it is a pony for him, which Billy will help him train. Carl, who cannot stand the expression of emotion, leaves the barn. The colt was bought for five dollars at a sale auctioning off the effects of a bankrupt traveling show. From this time on Jody always wakes before the breakfast signal and goes to see the colt, whom he named Gabilan, after the nearby mountains. Sometimes Billy Buck would be in the barn currying the work horses and would tell Jody all about the animals. Billy himself is known as a fine hand with horses; the narrative mentions that Billy always wins the stock trials. In the fall Billy begins to show the boy how to train the pony, and finally the time comes for the saddle and bridle. On Thanksgiving Day Jody can ride; rain comes for a week, but Jody keeps his colt dry in the box stall. One day the sun shines and Billy tells Jody it is all right to leave the horse out in the corral; it won't rain; even if it does, it won't hurt the colt and Billy promises to take the horse in if the weather changes. It starts raining hard while Jody is at school but trusting in Billy, Jody feels assured. Arriving home, he finds the worst has happened; Billy couldn't get back from his chores in time to get the soaking pony in out of the rain. Jody's rubbing doesn't stop the horse's shivering; Billy rubs him down too, but the colt gets worse. The next day Billy lets Gabilan breathe in a vapor to clear his respiration; it works a little. Jody omits his chores this night. In the morning Billy cuts a slash into a swelling in Gabilan' jaw and allows it to drain. It is Saturday, and Jody makes up a bed for himself in the hay. He keeps watch on his colt, but grows sleepy. At nine in the evening, he wakes in a panic and finds the colt outside in the wind. Billy comes in at dawn and opens a little hole in Gabilan's windpipe to help the colt breathe. Jody swabs the wound out during the morning. Carl enters, asks the boy to come away, and on receiving an angry objection from Billy, leaves hurt. Billy relieves the boy on watch for awhile. Jody takes over again and at daylight he wakes, springs up as he sees the door open and his horse gone. He follows the tracks and sees a circle of buzzards nearing the earth. Jody finds his colt but not before the first buzzard has rammed his beak into the dead colt's eye. Jody seizes the bird and kills it. Billy and Carl arrive; the father wipes the bird's blood off his son's face and tells him it wasn't the buzzard that killed Gabilan. But Billy Buck angrily says, "'Course he knows it ..." to his employer, and he accuses Carl of a lack of understanding.

The Dream

Although this section, like the next two, serves to introduce Jody to some aspect of death and significant loss, there is a particular quality in "The Gift" which expresses a sense of deprivation and doom. This is conveyed by a lyrical, almost dreamlike perception of nature and the processes of life. One series of incidents most particularly evokes this feeling. It involves Jody's journey to visit his new horse every morning. Significantly, the young boy breaks his routine for the first time in these early morning visits. Before the acquisition of the pony, Jody would rise when he was summoned. In other words, he responded to another person's sense of appropriateness. That he now gets up before he has to signifies the birth of a new feeling of responsibility; and more importantly, it signifies the genesis of a sense of self which is taking the boy Jody through the journey from childhood to maturity. He wakes before his mother wakes, the narrative tells us. So the world is the boy's, untrammeled by the authoritative presence of a parent. It is Jody's experience that counts. But sometimes one person does rise at this time-

Billy Buck, who curries the work horses very early if they are to be used that day. And it is Billy who serves as the boy's male ideal, not Carl Tiflin. The narrative describes Jody's trip to see his horse using words such as "strange," "mysterious," and "dream." Nature tends to take on human attributes; the stones are "sleeping"; the cypress tree is "sleeping." The world of the child can often be characterized by this animistic quality, a quality usually lost in maturity. In this, the beginning of Jody's path of knowledge of pain and death, the dreamlike sense of wonder and the marvellous gains its power from the fact that it is the first. However intense and varied later experiences may turn out to be, they will never again be first, a fact which has always given particular poignancy to early love, and-as in this case-early passages toward understanding the world. In this novella, as in many of Steinbeck's works, concrete particulars of a scene also symbolize some abstract qualities. The cypress tree, for instance, which is "sleeping" in Jody's early rising mornings later takes on overtones of menacing evil and suffering; it is the place where the pigs are scalded, and in future **episodes** rouses in the boy sensations of fear and disgust. He is too taken up with the magic of his present involvements to be aware of these now. In short, what causes a person to get up in the mornings is a clue to the quality of his life. If he rises eager, and out of love, no man can misread the portents. If he rises only because of duty, from which a sense of hope or optimism may be lacking, the direction of his life is different. This is not merely the story of a young boy; it suggests the life-long commitment of purpose and its possible twin, obligation.

The Reality

While the context of much of "The Gift" involves departures from strict "scientific" fact in the interest of lyrical and fantasy experience, it is interesting to note an important and universal paradox. The maturing journey, which involves ownership of the horse and responsibility for it, and in which Nature is a sweet accomplice, also focuses Jody's attention on the world of fact in an unexampled manner. Jody, who has been around horses all his life, sees one for the first time; he suddenly begins to notice the particularities of the flank muscles and the cords of the buttocks; he starts to interpret the subtle indications given by horses' ears by studying Gabilan's ears very closely. Drawn back in fear or anger, forward in pleasure and curiosity, a whole gamut of in-between positions can communicate Gabilan's state to a sharp observer. Besides the level of reality represented by such concerns, others press increasingly upon the boy Jody; the abstract realities of cause and effect, the sense of his own irrationality, and the reality of Billy Buck's fallibility. These pressures are all intermingled.

Jody

It is often said that the beginnings of a child's maturity are evident when he starts to doubt his parents' absolute dependability. As the child discovers his father is no hero, and finds flaws, he also begins to perceive essential imperfections in the world. The Irish poet William Butler Yeats said that a man does not start to live until he conceives of life as a tragedy. And this is what "The Gift" is all about. Whom can the boy blame for the death of his pony? What really caused Gabilan's death? Billy Buck had said that it wouldn't rain. A country man must live day by day, using his sense of the weather like all his other senses. He occasionally makes mistakes. As Jody's hero, Billy was not allowed to make mistakes. However, it is an indication of a character both healthy and affectionate that Jody did not utterly reject Billy after the ranch hand was found to have feet of clay. In any case, was it actually Billy's "fault" that the pony got sick? What part did Jody's own carelessness play in Gabilan's end? Would the pony have died even if Jody had not fallen asleep and allowed it to run loose, thus aggravating its condition? Jody, after all, had to sleep sometime and the very fact of his human need bore in itself the seed of the pony's death. None of these questions are answerable in any absolute or easy manner. Jody has come into a region of violence and arbitrary lack of understandable causality which Steinbeck holds is the beginning of wisdom. When he kills the buzzard who has just pecked out Gabilan's eye, he knows as well as anyone that the buzzard is no more to blame than anyone else for the wounding loss. This incident may also be interpreted as indicating a further instance of Jody's maturing-his development of meaningful values. The pony has quite obviously established itself high on Jody's hierarchy of values and the desecration of his pet by the buzzard would naturally evoke an emotional response from the boy. Even though the animal is dead, the scavenging of the bird would appear as destruction of a crucial value-wanton treatment of a physical body dear to Jody. Billy understands this, but not so Jody's father. Aside from these developmental considerations, we see Jody in the ordinary course of things as an extraordinarily well-disciplined boy, but one in whom parental authority has not stifled a strong and active fantasy life. He is clearly affectionate, although the relative formality of interpersonal relationships on the ranch does not give him much of a chance to express warmth often or overtly; indeed the long farm day-from the proverbial dawn to dusk-represents a world far different from the one more typical of the mid-twentieth century middle-class.

Billy Buck

The ranchhand is described as broad and bandylegged. He has a walrus moustache and muscled hands. His eyes - like

Jody's incidentally - are grey. He is a man immensely skilled in country arts. He understands animals as if he were one of them; his experience and self-confidence allow him to perform such operations as the tracheotomy on the pony; his capacity for self-regulation within the requirements of necessity are such that when he curries and brushes the work horses before breakfast, he finishes at the exact moment that it is time to go in to the ranch house for the meal. And this apparently petty trait is the clue to his importance, especially in Jody's development. Billy has come to recognize necessity, the duties involved in farm responsibilities; but he fulfills them in a spirit of quiet competence and real satisfaction, and sometimes in a spirit of authentic pleasure. In addition, he is the representative in this novella of Steinbeck's common hero figure: like the equally self-confident Slim - an excellent craftsman - in *Of Mice and Men*, Billy accepts reality in its complexities; he knows that death occurs in the midst of life; he knows that the buzzard belongs as clearly in the chain of being as the man and the horse, each to its appointed place. Through all this, he is a man capable of great compassion; much more than Carl Tiflin, Jody's father. Billy is able to allow the boy to grieve, and can put Jody's furious assault upon the buzzard in its proper psychological perspective.

Carl Tiflin

Jody's father is described in much less detail than Billy Buck, merely as "tall and stern." He is unable, not only to express emotion directly and simply, but also to let others project their feelings freely in his presence; underneath his self-protective brusqueness, he can be generous, as in his gift of the pony to his son, but he withdraws from intimate contact with others.

Mrs. Tiflin

Known as Mrs. Tiflin, or as "Jody's mother," she is a more or less generalized figure, working very hard in the ranch house, occupied with constant domestic detail. She runs her house efficiently, but does not suffer from the coldness that some kinds of efficiency seem to impart. Her attitude during Jody's ordeal is warm, understanding and permissive. She demonstrates these qualities not so much by overt behavior as by her tolerance of his sudden withdrawal from his chores, which are of importance to the domestic economy of the ranch.

Another look at Jody, The Major Character

The fact that Jody patterns himself after Billy Buck rather than his father suggests an interesting consideration. Particularly because of the lyrical and suggestive quality of some of the prose, and because of the universal aspect of the boy's adolescent passage, it is not irrelevant to remember the old and oft-repeated legends about the children and youths raised by one set of parents but in reality the offspring of kings or aristocrats. These stories generally emphasize the fact of an ancestry more romantic, more aristocratic, more importantly historical than one's own. In this sense, Jody's patterning himself after Billy Buck reveals a feeling about America often found in Steinbeck's work. Throughout his carreer, the novelist often discloses an aversion to values commonly associated with the middle-class, consisting primarily of that intensity of involvement with ownership and vested interest which he thought narrows the range of human sympathy. Steinbeck could not understand how a man overly concerned with the making and saving of money, the appropriation and aggrandizement of property, could give generously of himself, act spontaneously, or love the work he does-to act, in short, in the heroic mold of the old frontier explorers and travelers which he concretized in the personality of Billy Buck. However simplified, this sense of the American character of the past is nevertheless a reigning image in much of the novelist's work. The fourth section particularly, "The Leader of the People," will recall these speculations to the reader.

PART II: THE GREAT MOUNTAINS

Synopsis

This second **episode** begins with the boy Jody, bored on a hot midsummer afternoon, looking for something to do to break the monotony. He kills a thrush with a slingshot, then goes to his area of peace, mentioned in the synopsis of Part I, where he drinks from the mossy tub which catches the sweet spring water. Although the hills are dry and the grass straw-colored, there is fine green grass around the tub, where the water overflows; we remember this locale again and its symbolic stress upon life. Jody looks at the mountain ranges in the West and recalls questioning his parents and Billy about them He learned only about the inconceivable dryness there, the endless sequence of ridges reaching to the Pacific; they became objects of fascination, and of horror. He turns his head to the east, and sees the Gabilan Mountains, containing complexities of ranches, and long-enduring pine trees, and the memory of battles against the Mexicans. Suddenly the boy sees something.

It is a moving figure headed toward the house, an old man. He tells the embarrassed Jody his name is Gitano; he used to live there; he has come back. He tells Mrs. Tiflin he used to live in a little adobe house nearby, which has nearly been washed away; he has come back to die. Mr. Tiflin explains he cannot feed and clothe and care for an old man. Gitano can stay the night in the old bunkhouse, but then he must go, after breakfast. Jody shows the old man where he is to sleep. They talk. In response to the boy's passionate interest in the fact that the old paisano (of mixed Native American and Spanish descent) has been in the Great Mountains, all the visitor says is that they are "quiet ... nice." Jody, unable to leave the dying old man, shows him the stock in the barn. They look at old Easter, Carl Tiflin's first horse, now thirty years old, a walking relic. Carl walks over and says that it's a shame not to kill the old animal. Jody assures the paisano Mr. Tiflin was only "talking". Old Gitano rubs the horse's lean neck. The boy and the old man go in to supper; Gitano remains standing until invited formally to sit down. He tells the Tiflins he has relatives in Monterey, nearby; Carl suggests he go there; Mrs. Tiflin feels it is too bad the old man can't stay with them.

Jody thinks about the old man, mysterious as the Great Mountains, hiding his inner self behind his eyes. The boy wanders in the darkness toward the bunkhouse, pushes the door open, sees the visitor holding a beautifully carved rapier in his hand; Gitano cannot hide it in time. It is from his father, he tells the boy. What does he do with it? Nothing. He just keeps it. He lets Jody see it again. The boy leaves, knowing he must never tell anyone; there is a fragility in the truth represented by the sword. In the morning, old Easter is assumed dead: he hasn't come down to water with the other horses. But in mid-morning a neighbor comes with a story. He saw an old man on an old horse, unsaddled, cutting through the brush, carrying a shiny object. Carl checks his guns, none are missing. Jody walks up to the brush line near the house, and looks toward the Great Ones. For a moment he thought he could see a minute dot moving up there. He thought of the rapier, of Gitano, of the vast mountains.

He lay down in the green grass around the tub-indescribably unhappy, he lies there a long time, his eyes covered.

Gitano

The old paisano is described in a certain amount of detail as he first appears walking toward Jody's house. Although his age can be discerned at a distance by the way his heels strike the ground hard in a jerky manner, his figure is lean and straight. He wears jeans, clodhopper shoes and an old Stetson. He bears a lumpy sack on his back. His face is dark; he wears a moustache, white like his hair. He has a real old man's face, the skin enveloping the bones of the skull tightly but showing absolutely no wrinkles. His wrists are bony and strong, his nails flat and shiny. Gitano is identified with evening and with the Great Mountains, by Jody in any case. When the old man and the boy are looking at Easter, the sun sinking and the ranch quiet, Jody senses an equality between the old paisano and the mood of the night. And the brooding mystery of the Great Mountains is somehow transmuted into the monosyllabic, but pregnant, communications by Gitano. He is a living analogue of that more-than-human secret and awe-inspiring silence held by the Great Ones, a silence that neither the boy's father nor even Billy Buck can explain for Jody. The ranges become more than a geographical quality, a topographical rise; they assume the dark lineaments of the boy's own hoped-for and feared future and symbolize his yearnings about life beyond the boundaries of his own environment. The concept of the heroic American past, as mentioned in the previous Plot Synopsis, here gets a further emphasis in Gitano, whose name itself means "gypsy," or wanderer. The shiny rapier, completely at odds with the old man's clothes, condition of life, age and prospects, serves as a reminder of the reality of an excitement and an adventure and a heroism which constitute an antidote to the humdrum aspects of being "settled-down." Some critics have accused Steinbeck of so seriously damaging many of his stories by his gratuitous intrusion into them of such obviously symbolic incidents that the level of the narration can no longer engage the reader's intense attention or belief. The incident of Gitano's sword may seem to be near to absurdity, but in the context of Jody's brooding coming-of-age as expressed in Steinbeck's calmly lyrical prose the rapier certainly gathers around itself the halo of the boy's lust for historical and geographical glory.

The Carl Tiflin-Billy Buck Relationship

We have seen that of the two models of masculine behavior available to the boy he picks Billy rather than his father. In the first section Billy is depicted as a more understanding, more empathic individual than Carl. In this second part Billy still demonstrates a larger capacity for sympathy than his employer; however, another element now enters in and makes the reader react more favorably to Jody's father. On several occasions Billy disagrees with Carl and takes a more humanitarian direction. When Mr. Tiflin suggests that Easter be shot, Billy breaks in with the comment that "old things" have a right to rest after working all their lives. When Carl tells the ranchhand that the country's full "of these old paisanos," Billy defends them, claiming that they work better at a more advanced age than other men. But Carl's next remark is one with which Billy agrees, to which he gives his support: Carl reminds Billy how hard it is to keep the ranch solvent and out of the hands of the bank, how impossible it would be to take on anyone else in such a situation. Whereas Steinbeck usually downgrades propertied, day-to-day, obligatoried involvements, he presents them somewhat differently here in order to fill out his portrayal of a character, and to sympathetically explain what seem like hard-hearted and obdurate attitudes. Within this context, the reader senses that it is easier for Billy Buck to extend his sympathies to Gitano than it is for Carl, who bears the responsibility for keeping the little ranch group alive. In addition, the narrative suggests at several points that Carl's apparent hard-heartedness is largely the manifestation of a personal idiosyncracy, which does not permit the outward expression of warmth. Carl fears nostalgia, which he calls softness, and often acts in defense of this fear by demonstrating an exaggerated harshness. When he talks about old Easter, he reminisces about the horse's departed power and grace, after which he immediately reproaches himself for yielding to a moment of self-indulgent softness. It is just at that point that he repeats his suggestion that the horse be shot. Again, the narrative itself says that Carl was "afraid" he might relent. Jody is represented as being aware of "how mean" his father felt for not allowing Gitano to stay.

Nature and Animal Symbolism

The reader will recall the weather typical of the first section: rain, storm, wind; the season of the first section is winter, of the second, midsummer. Steinbeck will sometimes imply an accord between weather and season on the one hand and narrative action on the other. This principle is generally operative in these two sections, the first concerned with the violent and sudden shock of death, the second a representation of old age and death so calm, peaceful and symbolic as to exist with perfect congruity in the context of the quiet and hanging heat of the summer. The reader will remember more symbolism drawn from analogous sources. The Great Mountains, or Great Ones, which give this section its title, are radically different from the Gabilan Mountains. It is ironic that the red pony of the initial **episode** should have been given the name of that range of mountains which represents life, a sense of settled community, a concept of familiarity. The Great Ones, on the other hand, represent the mystery of the unknown, the looming fear of the dry and the dark. Another symbolic feature familiar to the reader of Steinbeck consists of the direct or indirect comparison of man to animals, which critics have deplored as an insult to the integrity of these qualities which make human beings peculiarly themselves - and which the novelist's defenders point to as techniques demonstrating Steinbeck's deep sympathy for the natural order, and for natural processes, of which man, however superior, is but a part. An example of this kind of comparison may be found in the Gitano-Easter coupling. (The novel *Of Mice and Men* also contains, for instance, a comparison between an old man and a dying dog in such a way as to leave no doubt of the author's symbolic intention.) Carl's gross verbal emphasis on the parallel in Gitano's presence by no means exhausts the suggestiveness of the comparison. Where the rancher uses the concept in order to insure the departure of the old paisano, the comparison also serves to remind the reader of the old man's spent youthful grace and strength, of the essential poetic identity between man and the other members of the animal kingdom.

Jody

We may note the contrast in Jody's reactions to his two losses. His response to the death of the red pony was physical, violent as well as verbal. This was a loss which involved the entire ranch in an active and shared manner. Billy Buck passionately tried to help as much as he could; Jody's mother was constantly, if quietly, aware; Jody's father, however masked his feelings, reacted as well to the death of the little colt. But for Jody the loss of Gitano was less personal than symbolic and universal;

no doubt the boy had some sense in the first section that the buzzard was fulfilling his appointed role by attacking the flesh of the dead horse, but that hardly constituted Jody's essential reaction. In the second part, however, Jody's loss is a "nameless" sorrow, less a specific relating than generalized feeling of the immensity of the past, that vast imprecise period in which the conquistadores (Spanish colonizers of America) brought such swords as that which Gitano carries to his death in the Great Ones.

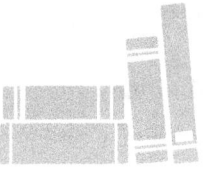

THE RED PONY

TEXTUAL ANALYSIS

PARTS III AND IV

PART III: THE PROMISE

Synopsis

This third section takes place in the spring time. Like the second part, it opens with Jody acting like a typical country-patterned ten-year-old. He leads an imaginary army home from school, hunts imaginary game, and collects toads, lizards, snakes, grasshoppers and a newt. Once home, he hears from his mother that his father and Billy Buck are waiting to talk to him. Carl Tiflin offers Jody the chance to raise a colt; the father will put up the five dollar stud fee for Nellie the mare, and Jody will have to work it off during the coming summer. Jody is ecstatic and deeply grateful to Billy, whose intercession is mentioned by Carl as an important element in giving the boy this present. The next morning Jody, bearer of a five-dollar bill wrapped in a piece of newspaper and pinned to a pocket inside his overalls, takes the mare to the stud farm to meet the stallion. After an hour of uphill trudging, Nellie suddenly rears; the stallion roars down the hill, kicked at by the mare as he whizzes by; he strikes her with the front hoof. She suddenly becomes coy and rubs against the stallion. At this point, Jess Taylor, the horse's owner, arrives. He suggests that Jody go to the house and get a piece of pie; the boy refuses and insists on leading the mare up. After the stallion has serviced the mare, Jody takes her home, where he becomes a virtual slave for the late spring and summer, paying off his father for the stud fee. One day, three months after the incident at Jess Taylor's, Bill Buck and Jody go to look at Nellie; Jody thinks she hasn't changed. Billy tells the boy it'll be five months before he sees a sign, eight months more before the mare gives birth, and about two years more before Jody will be able to ride. Billy then tells the boy how the mares give birth; sometimes if the colt is in the wrong position the mare needs help; a man should be around at that time. Jody pleads with Billy to be around: they both remember Gabilan. Jody waits, sometimes filling the days with heroic fantasies of himself and his new horse. In September he notices Nellie's stomach swollen. On the night of February second, already later than the forecast time, Jody walks at night to the mare's stall. Billy, in the hayloft, tells the boy to go home; everything will be all right. Jody goes to sleep, but is soon awakened roughly; it is Billy: Nellie is ready. The mare strains, is wrung in a spasm. The foal is turned wrong. Billy is unable to turn it for a proper exit from the birth canal. Desperate, he reaches for a heavy horseshoe hammer with his wet right hand; he tells Jody to leave, but the boy is willing only to turn his face. There is a crunch of bone; the boy sees the hammer fall on Nellie's forehead. Sawing and ripping at the tough belly, Billy finally manages to get the little black colt out. He walks over and puts it on the straw at Jody's feet. His face and arms red with blood, his body shivering, Billy in an almost unhearable voice tells the boy he's fulfilling his obligation; the Colt is there as Billy had promised. Jody is still too stunned by the situation to do anything except stare dumbly at the little animal. Billy has to shout at him to get hot water and a sponge to clean the foal. The boy finally goes out, but haunted by the look of Billy, and the sight of the blood.

Billy Buck

Logically, the ranchhand's move in killing the mare and saving the foal is certainly unexpected. In the course of a conversation with Jody early in this section, Billy had been talking about how things can go wrong when mares give birth. He told the boy that sometimes the colt has to be torn to pieces to get it out, or else the mare will die. This procedure seems reasonable, since a mare can give birth again; a colt on the other hand, takes years to grow to adulthood, and besides, of course, may be male. Why did Billy then choose to save the colt? The answer is probably a compound of at least two elements. First, there is no doubt that Billy's image of himself is to some degree influenced by the way Jody looks at him. This is not to say that the characteristics of independence and craftsmanship for which Billy is known would not exist in another, similar, context. But the novelist does suggest, subtly, that influences, particularly if they are intense and significant, and leading to action, are usually reciprocal-even in the case of a boy and a man. After all, a father is a man who has a son, and is thus defined in terms of someone other than himself. That Billy is very sensitive to his lowered status in Jody's eyes is a fact that cannot escape the reader; the narrative makes a point of it throughout *The Red Pony*. There is a second point, closely related of course to the first: Billy loves the boy. And those months of waiting, during which he was continuously and sympathetically attuned to Jody's anxieties and excitements about the mare's condition, dictated his choice. The logic of stock-breeding may have suggested that Nellie be saved, at the expense of the colt;

but the logic of love ordered differently. It is well to bear in mind the probably intense struggle that went on in the ranchhand's mind in that split second during which the decision was made; for Billy's entire training and experience with animals were tremendously strong forces which under almost any other circumstances would have directed him to the other choice.

Jody: The Cypress and The Tub

We have seen that the first two sections of this novella have mentioned, in passing, Jody's short trips behind the house, to the brush line; there the old wooden tub caught the fresh spring water, and there the grass surrounding the old tub was always green. There has also been brief mention of the cypress tree by the bunkhouse, and Jody's dislike for it. In this section, "The Promise," these two symbols are treated directly and fully in the narrative. We learn that the place with the tub had come to be a focal point for the boy. When punished, he is soothed by the quietly flowing water and the grass; when feeling mean, he can lose his meanness in the calm security of the brush line. The obstacles and assaults of the day do not exist there. For instance, at one point, Jody's anxious pleas for the future welfare of his colt touch Billy Buck in a vulnerable place, for he knows that the boy is thinking about what happened to the red pony. Jody, upset by this remembrance, and disturbed all the more by finding himself under the black cypress tree he hates, goes to the tub to be soothed and cleansed of tensions. And it is at this time that he engages in his most intense fantasying about himself and his grown-up horse, called in his imagination Black Demon. The cypress tree, on the other hand, symbolizes death and pain to the boy. The pigs came there to be slaughtered, after which they were scalded in a big iron kettle and the skins scraped. (It is interesting in this connection to observe that Steinbeck says that although these slaughters so upset the boy that he took refuge in his tub spot, Jody nevertheless found the process "fascinating." One of the main reasons for the success of these **episodes** lies in the novelist's insistence on not sentimentalizing the nature of boyhood.) The importance of these two major symbols in the developing continuity of the boy's life pertains to the seriousness of the stage which the boy has now reached. The first **episode** dealt with the little red pony's increasing ill-health and eventual death; the second with an old man's symbolic search for a place to die; here the reader finds an **episode** concerning itself with a birth, a new life, not an exhausted one. We sense that nothing important is gained easily; besides the heartache attendant to the mare's necessary death, we do not forget that this colt, unlike the red pony, had to be paid for by arduous and new tasks and chores during the spring and the entire summer. The boy did them willingly, but would have had to in any case. The implicit struggle between the qualities represented by the tub and the cypress reflects the new level of maturity and understanding reached by Jody by the end of this section. Life is gotten by sacrificing life, but the new life will probably prosper. The struggle never ends: the buzzards will continue eating carrion; horses will get sick and die; old men must leave the earth; brood mares may have to be sacrificed; but after it all, the new life - the colt's and, in a poetically suggestive way, Jody's too - does come into its own, with a future bravely hopeful.

PART IV: THE LEADER OF THE PEOPLE

Synopsis

It is a Saturday in March; Billy Buck is raking together the remainder of last year's haystack. What's left after the raking is tainted by ground moisture. Jody is pleased at the possibility of hunting for mice with the dogs. For eight months the mice have multiplied in the haystack, protected from their enemies; now, fat and well-fed, they are the boy's prey. Billy reminds the boy to get permission from his father, who wants to be consulted on all doings on the ranch, big or small. Carl Tiflin suddenly comes down the road to the house; he has a letter from his father-in-law, who writes that he is coming to visit for a little while and is due this very day. The news makes Carl unhappy: the old man gets on his nerves with incessant references to the departed glory of the old days, a period of heroic adventure. During the period of westward expansion in the United States, Mrs. Tiflin's father was a leader of groups of voyagers and pioneers who had made the long, difficult and dangerous trek. Mrs. Tiflin tries to elicit from her husband a sympathetic concern for her father whose life had derived its meaning from his leadership, for whom the Pacific Ocean represented a barrier to further travel and a cessation of significant action. Carl remains irritated and stalks out. Jody goes to greet the old man on the road leading to the ranch. The boy invites the grandfather to join him on a mouse hunt the next day; the response is kind but evasive. From the door Mrs. Tiflin waves her apron in welcome; Carl Tiflin goes to the house for the greeting. Billy Buck is hurrying to the house too, after having shaved - an unusual act for a Saturday - but Billy reveres Grandfather. Soon everyone is seated at the supper table, and the old man settles insensibly into his usual pattern of telling the old stories again and again. Carl interrupts the Grandfather on several occasions, earning his wife's anger both at supper and afterward in front of the fireplace. No one but Jody responds when the old man asks if the company wishes to hear a particular story. Jody then asks Grandfather to tell about Native Americans. Carl tries to turn the conversation into other channels; it doesn't work. Before going to bed Jody asks permission to kill the mice the next day. It is granted. He rises before the breakfast signal the next day to make a mouse-killing flail. He tells Billy those mice don't know what will happen to them this day; neither does anyone else, Billy responds, an answer which "staggers" the boy. At breakfast Carl is angry and complains that the past is done with, nobody wants to hear the same stories again and again. Grandfather walks in, smiling tightly. Carl asks if he has heard. Upon receiving an affirmative response, Carl apologizes. The old man says he doesn't mind what was said; he is concerned only with the possibility that Carl's comment might be true: that he wouldn't like. Jody asks the old man if he wants to go hunt the mice; no, he'd rather sit in the sun. Jody's enthusiasm fails him; he returns to the old man, who tries to explain: it is not the stories that really matter, but the feeling responses from people that count. People will never really understand how it was in the old days, the huge mass going West. Jody suggests he himself might lead the people some day. The old man smiles: there is no place to go; every place is taken; it is finished. The drive Westward is stopped permanently by the Pacific. Carl is right, the old man tells Jody, who feels very sad and offers the Grandfather a glass of lemonade made by himself. He goes to the kitchen to get a lemon from his mother, who is very touched to see that he does not want one for himself.

Grandfather

He wears a black broadcloth suit and a black tie. His collar is short and hard. His hat is black, his beard white, eyebrows white, eyes blue. In general his stance is one of great dignity; his motion has no hesitancy. His eyes at one point are described as "stern, merry"; these adjectives are utilized during his first conversation with Jody, when the boy invites him to hunt mice the next day. The reader here notes a very important element in the relationship between the old man and his grandson. It is often said that sympathy skips a generation, or even that character traits do so. It is inconceivable that Jody would at any time have invited his father to hunt mice. Of course the relationship between a man and his grandson, precisely because of the lack of constant responsibility, often demonstrates more permissiveness than that between a father and son. But beyond this, Grandfather exhibits a particular capacity for entering seriously into the games of a child, without dismissing these games as unimportant or trifling. Such a capacity for play often distinguishes individuals of imagination. No leader can exercise his will, and hold together a mass of disparate individuals, without imagination. And it is the imaginative aspects of the march Westward whose loss Grandfather so intensely and continuously deplores. In spite of his constant emphasis on this loss, the old man is curiously detached, not lacking in interest in the world but removed from its petty concerns, as a man with a dream is perhaps immune to much triviality. When he tells one of his stories, for instance, the narrative mentions the fact that the blue eyes were "detached," that the old man looked as if he were not very interested in the story himself. Sometimes the power of a conviction is such that the individual experiences his commitment as a force outside of himself. That is what the Grandfather means when he states that he does not care about the stories themselves, he cares only about the great truth in which his stories have their existence: the truth about the pioneering spirit and the sacrifice and the risk. Interestingly, Grandfather's passionate involvement with that spirit does not blind him to the excesses perpetrated by the troops which hunted Native Americans and in the process shot children and burnt teepees. He goes out of his way to make this point to his grandson. Another proof of the old man's lack of pettiness or vindictiveness manifests itself when Jody boasts about how much he has grown since the previous year. Grandfather makes a kind of folksy remark suggesting that much of that growth is water; one would have to wait till the boy "heads out" before analyzing the quality of that growth. But in this remark, which in Carl Tiflin's mouth might very well have involved a "putting-in-your-place," the boy senses absolutely no rancor, no "will to injure." This is why Jody trusts Grandfather, who treats him with the sober courtesy to which a boy will usually react favorably. And the reader is touched and amused by the incongruousness created by Jody's use of "sir" at the same time he gravely tells the old man about the death of Riley, the nice pig, who died when a haystack fell on top of him.

Grandfather and The Moth

Steinbeck's fiction often contains short paragraphs or anecdotes deriving their substance from the world of animal nature. These anecdotes seem frequently to play the part of parables and act as symbolic analogues to set off some part of the narrative action. In this section the reader finds an interesting use of such a paragraph, intercalated in between conversational segments when the family is having supper together. Grandfather has just gone into one of his typical and apparently endless recitations, his voice assuming the special quality he reserves for his stories of the old times. Suddenly a big moth enters the room, and circles the kerosene lamp. Billy Buck tries to kill it by clapping it between both hands, but he fails; Carl Tiflin strikes with one cupped palm and catches the moth, after which he breaks it. Right after this **episode** Grandfather begins again, but is immediately interrupted by Carl who tells him to eat more meat, since the others are all ready for pudding. This incident may suggest implicitly the ambivalent symbolic nature of Grandfather. On the one hand he represents the aspects of the past, of national history whose memory fertilizes the present; on the other, Grandfather and the nostalgia he stands for have to die. The old man is represented as extremely sympathetic in this narrative, as we have seen. But Carl does not become a devil figure in consequence. After all, Jody's father does have a job to do, he does it well, and if it does not glory in the radiance of treks to the West, it nevertheless is involved in the consolidation of gains stemming from the earlier period. To a significant degree, it is Grandfather who can not adjust himself to a different world, who lives more in illusion than his son-in-law. When imagination becomes illusion is a point difficult to isolate, and it is this difficulty that contributes to the poignancy of the figure of the old man, and to the aptness of Carl's harsh symbolic action in "breaking" the moth, whose need to fly near the light costs it its life.

Jody

The boy shows great compassion and mature courage in this section of the narrative. In the beginning of the **episode**, his mother and father call him Big-Britches when the boy rushes to his mother to be the first to tell her of the coming of the letter. After his father's cruel statement that the family had indeed heard such-and-such stories many times. Jody takes it upon himself to ask his Grandfather to "tell about Indians." He says it softly, with no intent to provoke his father or placate his mother. He wants only to make the old man happy, to salve this wounded ego. Jody, the narrative tells us, knows exactly how his Grandfather feels, empty inside. Had the boy himself not undergone the same kind of belittling before, in the Big-Britches **episode**? But here Jody is certain that what he is doing is morally right. He does not stop at this point either, because directly after this he is the only one to encourage the old man again. The particular bond between the old man and his grandson is emphasized when the Grandfather tells him that the taming of the wilderness was a job for men but that only boys want to hear about it nowadays. In fact the boy's sympathy for the old man is such that the mice - those nice fat potential victims of the first part of this **episode** - are still around at the end. The play instinct and the hunting instinct are suppressed in deference to a recognition of the old man's life quandary.

The 'Group Man' Theory

The reader will recall some discussion of Steinbeck's *Sea of Cortez* in the Introduction. In this book, a survey of invertebrate marine life written in conjunction with a marine biologist, the novelist writes about the behavior of large numbers of tiny organisms making up one whole, whose activities and reactions differ qualitatively from a simple summation of individual members' traits. In this connection, it is interesting to note that Grandfather's longest statement recalls this concept to the reader. Indeed the statement is not only the longest, but, placed strategically near the end of this **episode**, it is in a way the old man's epitaph.

He speaks lyrically of The Experience, and of the sea that ended it. He tells Jody that the bunch of people who went West were really "one big crawling beast," of which he was the head; if not he, another would have been the head. "The thing" had to have a head. This **allusion** to a super-individual organism which has almost a will transcending the individuals composing it can be recognized as very typical of Steinbeck's thought, and is given narrative **exposition** in his later work.

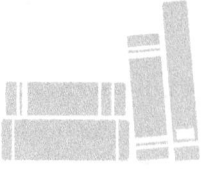

THE RED PONY

CHARACTER ANALYSES

Jody

The ten-year old son of the Tiflins, small ranch-owners. The four parts of *The Red Pony* detail the increasing acuity of his moral perception, a level of growth much more important than any spurts in physical size, which occur too. It is interesting that Steinbeck shaped the novella into its final form after the first, three-part, publication of *The Red Pony*. By making "The Leader of the People" an intrinsic part of his story the novelist constructed a symmetrical whole. The form he derived from this addition creates in the final version an alternating series of life adventures for the boy Jody. Where the first and third **episodes** are concerned with the boy's realistic and symbolic involvements with horses, the second and fourth deal with Jody's attitudes toward two old men, each representative of a lost past. Parts I and III disclose a clear advance in Jody's maturity. Whether Parts II and IV actually represent an increase in moral awareness is a difficult point to ascertain. Though informed by a symmetry on the basis suggested above, the novella is, after all, not a mathematical equation, with equal and consistent spiritual "advancement" characterizing every segment. In any case life itself will not manifest continuous and successive movements of growth. Some periods are fallow, some germinal; and they may appear in unexpected combinations, at unforeseen periods. Insofar as the first and third parts are concerned, the loss of the show pony Gabilan does seem to be experienced on a lower level of moral perception than the loss of the mare Nellie; the regret for death is not the same as the celebration of life, and the latter specifically defines the quality of the third **episode**, haunted though it is by Jody's awareness of Billy's blood-stained face and hands. In the first part, the boy has lost something, a possession which he had made no great effort to obtain in the first place. In the third segment, the loss of Nellie is experienced rather as the loss of a link in a chain of transmission, involving a conception of the chain as a whole. Thus these two **episodes** suggest that only morally satisfying ownership is that in which the object and animal owned has been the cause of some personal abnegation or sacrifice, and it is also that in which the emotive and ethical life of the owner has become a real element of being. These considerations receive some support from Steinbeck's known attitudes toward the middle-class ethos, of which ownership of goods, moneys and property is for him the crucial essence. Thus what redeems the incursions into other lives is necessarily a sacrificial act, an exchange of some significant sort-which also brings us to a particularly Steinbeckian concept, the interrelationship of all forms of life and the impersonal, apparently cruel processes of the evolutionary fact. As for the **episodes** in which the boy Jody is involved with the old paisano Gitano and the old Grandfather, they bear many parallels. The boy in both cases is drawn outside of himself to acts of compassion and generosity. With old Gitano, Jody takes it upon himself to show the visiting paisano the stock in the barn, and, unlike the father, to treat him with deference and honor. It can be objected that Jody's generosity is not without a mixture of self-interest: after all Gitano is to him a possible key to the mystery of the Great Mountains. But after all one does not require or expect the behavior of a saint. And the boy's gratuitous acts of generosity toward the Grandfather are not without their personal involvements. At one point Jody says to the old man, "Maybe I could lead the people some day," a statement which is a compound of both respect and love and that kind of intense personal involvement which is the desire for emulation.

Billy Buck

The physical details are few and clear; they have been alluded to before - the walrus moustache, the small stature, the square hands, the eyes grey as Jody's - Billy Buck, the ranchhand, represents more than any other character in this novella the kind of man who is often featured as the hero in Steinbeck's work. Those categories in which Billy conforms to the general type of the hero involve the quality of his professional commitments and the cast of his thought. Billy Buck resembles such archetypal characters as Slim in *Of Mice and Men* in his expertise; the reader is told quite early that there is very little Billy Buck does not know about farm animals, about the needs of a ranch. Billy is characterized by the double capacities for objectivity and compassion. He understands more clearly than the other **protagonists** that everything that lives belongs in the large evolutionary order; that buzzards and boys, regardless of the value projected on either by human beings, each fulfill certain purposes. His perception of the paradoxical realities of life are essentially humanized by his ability to sympathize with the needs-sometimes unverbalized-of boys like Jody and old men like Gitano and Grandfather. Awareness of tragedy does not preclude sympathy; it does not make the ranchhand hard or rigid or humorless. In addition, Billy's roots are disclosed in the narrative. The reader gets no information about Carl's ancestry, but we know that Billy's father packed mules, that Grandfather knew him, and that he liked him. Thus the past nobility represented by Grandfather is reflected in Billy.

Carl Tiflin

Jody's father, the owner of the ranch, is dependable. We know him essentially through the experiences of his son. And in those experiences perhaps his main character trait involves his profound disinclination to "wear his heart on his sleeve." To his son he is a man of rules who will brook no disobedience or thwarting of will; he is also, beyond the granitic law-giver aspect of his temperament, a man who loves his son and would avoid any appearance of "softness" in the fear that his son should inherit a lack of hardihood. Such intense emotional austerity may portend certain quirks of character, or they may suggest merely certain cultural attitudes which look extreme only in the light of contemporary American culture. The infrequent mention of his relationship with other ranchers indicates that he is on good terms with his peers.

Mrs. Tiflin

She is almost a composite of certain abstract virtues rather than a fully developed character. Perhaps Steinbeck saw her as primarily the fulfiller of certain "feminine" roles in the rather traditional context of the small ranch presented in *The Red Pony*. Or perhaps she is merely another instance of the frequent female characters in the novelist's work, characters who do not often rise to a specific individuality usually reserved for the male protagonists. Mrs. Tiflin cooks, cleans, takes care, demonstrates quiet sympathy. She departs from these prototypical aspects only in the manifestation of her irritation at her husband for not behaving in a more kindly and tolerant manner toward Mrs. Tiflin's father. In this connection, the narrative tells us, she is even capable of expressing threatening overtones in her conversation. In keeping with the behavorial pattern on this ranch there is no direct expression, either physical or verbal, of affection between her and her husband. This fact, of course, is not to be taken as a statement that such affection is non-existent.

Gitano

The old paisano who comes a long way to die in what he considers a traditionally appropriate place, the area of the Tiflin ranch, near where he was born, in a now washed-away adobe shack. He is a man of gaunt, ascetic and immensely dignified appearance, lean and straight. For Jody, he is the very incorporation of the mystery of the past and of the mystery represented by the Great Mountains to the West, which originally had to be crossed to reach the Pacific, and which represent danger, aridity and the dangers peculiar to any great and significant crossings - thus they are somehow linked up in the boy's mind with the transition between his childhood and maturity, another great and significant crossing. Logically then Gitano, whose importance in this novella is directly proportional to the interest Jody takes in him, also symbolizes the elements of danger, traditionalism and fierce dignity which so deeply penetrate the heart of the boy.

Grandfather

Like Gitano, he is old, and also like Gitano he communicates a sense of traditionalism and dignity and a symbolic stance of the old times. The paradox of his situation lies in the fact that he can communicate a sense of the importance and heroism of the past only to a boy whose idealistic and fantasy-full imagination is precisely what marks him off from most men, who must struggle in the pragmatic and problem-ridden context of daily life for continuity and survival. Billy Buck has the ability to sympathize with the repeated tales of the old times and the frontier that emanate endlessly from the old man, but even Billy does not and can not listen when a story is told for the twentieth time. His "listening" is a matter of courtesy, not of real interest. Perhaps only Gitano, whom Grandfather never meets, could have understood almost intuitively the old man's passionate need for the transmission of the emotional experience which the pioneer marches exemplified for him. One of Grandfather's most endearing traits is his capacity to enter into the fantasy life of a ten-year old boy, without interposing the specious barrier of an adulthood reft of games and the pleasures of games. But the old man is also very vulnerable, and the possibility that the memories which constitute the importance of his life might be seen as illusions has a possibly devastating effect upon his sense of himself. How deeply he is wounded by his son-in-law's irritations and intolerances the reader does not really know, but that he experiences a sad and sudden reverse in his sense of reality can never be in doubt.

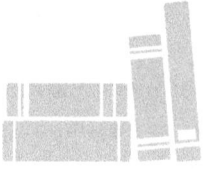

THE PEARL

TEXTUAL ANALYSIS

CHAPTERS I–III

CHAPTER I

Synopsis

This first Chapter, like Part I of *The Red Pony*, gives ample evidence of Steinbeck's long-time interest in the play form. *The Pearl*, of course, is not a stage drama; we might call it a novella, the category into which we also fitted *The Red Pony* - a piece of fiction longer than a long short story, but shorter than a novel; it runs some fifty-odd pages in length. The categorical definitions are somewhat arbitrary. Novels, after all, have been known-like those of Marcel Proust the 20th century French writer - to run to thousands of pages. So by novella, we merely mean a short novel. We mentioned the dramatic aspect of the narrative in order to point out that the major characters have all been introduced in the very beginning of the story, a procedure followed by a great many, if not indeed most playwrights. Kino, a South American native, probably of Bolivia though the country is never named in the narrative, wakes at dawn in his little house, really a kind of hut made mostly of brush. He sees his wife and young son Coyotite - an infant sleeping in hanging box. He also is aware of the water nearby: the noise of waves. His wife, Juana, takes care of the child, makes the morning cakes of corn. They speak only once, not feeling the need for verbal communication. A sun beam falls upon the baby's box and discloses a scorpion moving slowly down one of the suspension ropes. Juana mutters an ancient magic and then a Hail Mary. The child reaches up to the scorpion; Kino stands perfectly still; the child, laughing, shakes the rope and the scorpion falls, striking the baby in the shoulder. Kino mashes up the animal, but too late.

The mother sucks hard at the wound, spits out and sucks again to remove the poison. The baby is screaming and the neighbors run from their houses. Juana asks Kino to get the doctor, a most unusual request, for the community of brush houses never had the use of a doctor, whose practice consisted of people with enough money to pay for care. When he tells her the doctor would not come, she insists on going to his home. There is a great procession to the doctor's house. Kino, furious and fearful at confronting the symbol of those who had oppressed his people for four hundred years, gets up enough courage to knock at the door. The messenger returns: has Kino any money? The young man removes a creased paper containing eight poor quality pearls; the messenger takes it and comes back very soon, saying that the doctor is out, gone to call on a serious case. The reader by now knows definitely something that Kino merely suspects: the doctor is indeed home, irritated at being bothered by penniless natives. Kino puts his hat back on and strikes the gate such a crushing blow that his knuckles split and the blood flows between his fingers.

The Natural World

Not surprisingly, the world of this novella is characterized by the disinherited, the helpless, the exploited. (The reader will recall the Nobel Prize citation reproduced at the end of the Introduction.) It is also a non-urban world which, like *The Red Pony*, is populated with a variety of animal life. Steinbeck makes the narrative quite specific when he deals with details of such rural things as making a fire, particularities of animals, natural environment. For instance, he does not simply say that Juana builds a fire; we learn that she first goes to the fire pit, uncovers a coal, fans it aflame and breaks small pieces of brush over it. The menagerie of animals in this first Chapter includes roosters whose crowing occurs at the beginning of the novella, pigs ceaselessly digging among twigs and pieces of wood to find overlooked things to eat, little birds who "chittered and flurried." These are the sounds to which Kino wakes. Soon after that a "late moth" wanders in to find the fire, a thin dog comes over to Kino and lies down. One passing incident involving animal **imagery** is worth the reader's closer attention. As in *The Red Pony* and many of his other works, Steinbeck illustrates or counterpoints some particular element by the introduction of an **episode** taken from the world of animals, so in this first Chapter too we see a similar procedure. While he waits for breakfast, Kino watches the ants on the ground; typically, by the way, we find that there are two kinds of ants. Apparently there is warfare between these two types. The ant lion sets a sand trap for a little ant, which attempts frantically to get free of it. All this Kino watches "with the detachment of God." It is, he knows, simply part of the eternal struggle for survival characteristic of all animal life. He is outside of it, could settle the issue by one stamp of the foot, but decides to do nothing. But by, the end of this very Chapter-a short one at that-Kino himself is trying frantically, and unsuccessfully, to emerge from the trap that is the other side of his idyllic existence. Man is also an animal.

Ritual and Repetition

The environment in which Kino, his family and their neighbors live is what the anthropologists call a traditionalist society. Such a society is usually characterized as having minimal literacy, a hierarchy in which people find their place from birth and from which they rarely exit. Such societies, obviously, and particularly in comparison with the much more familiar mobile and changeful Western societies, can easily be found lacking in what the West holds important: literacy, equal suffrage, possibility of upward mobility, and equality before the law. But they are also characterized by some aspects peculiar to themselves. Significant among these is a delight in hallowed repetition, rather than a pleasure in change and an expectation of constant discoveries and excitements. The entire process of Kino's rising has a quality which can hardly be communicated by a mere statement of the plot. What he sees when he gets up is what he saw yesterday and what he would like to be able to see tomorrow. There is no hint of dissatisfaction, of a desire for "something better." The morning itself, for instance, taken as a whole, was morning "like other mornings," yet it is also "perfect among mornings." The breakfast that Kino eats is the traditional breakfast of himself and his people. The narrative points out that he has never had anything else for his first meal except on feast days and on one other occasion. Such unvaried custom would make very few advertising agencies prosper; such agencies are an intrinsic part of a culture in which the wish for something different permeates the daily life of the population, on whatever level one might investigate it.

The Parable

Steinbeck introduces his narrative with a short, two-paragraph italicized segment. In it he informs the reader, in vaguely Biblical prose, that the forthcoming story is a parable-from which everyone may take his own meaning. But he also mentions the fact that in a parable it is the universality of the meaning which is important, as well as the fact that old and retold tales tend to obliterate the subtle distinctions between definitions of good and evil, black and white. The dictionary defines the word parable in terms of simple stories bearing a clearly moral burden, often allegorical. Many critics might suggest that Steinbeck's introductory statement is not so much a notice of the use of a particular from as an overt recognition by the novelist-a deliberately specific recognition of a tendency clearly, if not formally, marked in much of the novelist's work. He has often been accused of scanting his character portrayals; of supplying, in an age of psychological complexity, two-dimensional banalities instead of dynamic integrations of character. Obviously an age of psychoanalysis will tend to find weaknesses in fiction unmarked by the "depth approach" in the building of character. The use of parable, of course, is tied in with certain cultural directions. The allegorical form is much more typical of, say, the Middle Ages than it is of the modern period. The form tends to be tied to cultures characterized by great simplifications, not simplicities. Craftsmen of the medieval period, for instance, were not as concerned as we are to create some original work. Their subjects tended to be very similar time and again, as any tour of medieval paintings featuring the Virgin and Child will prove. Thus the ritualistic aspects set forth in the preceding paragraph come into play in this context, which now becomes clearer. In this story the breakfast, the clothes, the breakfast food, the composition of the houses, the familial relationships all belong to a tradition at least, we are told, four hundred years old - and probably more. The intermingling of all these elements come together for Kino in what he calls the

THE RED PONY AND THE PEARL

Song of the Family, a quiet internal chant which tokens security, tranquility and peace. There is another Song which also makes its appearance in this first Chapter, the Song of the Enemy, or Song of Evil, which enters for the first time when the scorpion is glimpsed on the rope. Through these songs we get another insight into the particular tribal nature of Kino's society.

Kino

He is described only in rather general terms, being young, strong, dark of eye, brown in skin tone. His hair is black, his eyes are "warm and fierce," his moustache is thin. From the analysis of four beggars who roost constantly in front of the church in town - and watch as the pair brings the infant Coyotito to the doctor - the reader learns that Kino's clothes have been washed a thousand times, that his blanket is very old. His primary impulses appear to be based on his intense devotion to this wife and child. His awareness of enemy or evil almost seems to make no distinctions between animal or person or group. When he is about to knock on the doctor's door, he hears the Song of the Enemy; we are told earlier, in the scorpion incident, that the Song of Evil represents any foe of the family, that it is the music of the enemy. He is completely unaffiliated with any part of the white man's world, and the reader senses, even this early in the tale, that any adventure awaiting Kino outside of his carefully contrived environment may well be as deadly to him as air to fish.

Juana

Juana we know mostly through one of Kino's meditations about her. We know that she is apparently fearless in the service of her family. Kino tells us, in addition, that he often wondered at the "iron" in his patient and delicate wife. Notwithstanding her cheerfulness, she hardly cried out when giving birth. And her husband himself thinks that his wife is able to stand tiredness and hunger almost better than he himself. In a canoe she was "like a strong man." Such praise could hardly be more significant, because the reader learns later that the canoe is the one essential and valuable object that Kino owns.

The Doctor

We do not know his name. That in itself is an interesting fact. The reader will recall the brief discussion of allegory in a preceding paragraph; in that form, the characters will often be named according to the universal character, virtue, vice or other abstraction that they represent. Thus: Mr. Christian, Good-deeds, Castle Perilous, Slough of Despond, Mr. Worldly-Wiseman. Though Steinbeck hardly goes this far, he does present his Doctor as a kind of generalized symbol of particular characterological aspects, and as a symbol of some of the worst features of European civilization. He runs physically true to the type of middle-class, venal, manipulative, unethical, moneyed and propertied individual who is often portrayed in the novelist's work: all these vices often find a summation in one feature, fatness. And this Doctor is fat, so much so that when he lifts his delicate eggshell china cup to drink his fingers must be consciously spread out of the way so that he can grasp his cup with the remaining two. His eyes rest in "puffy little hammocks of flesh." His dressing gown, of red silk, and a prize from Paris, is now tight if he buttons it. His voice is hoarse with the fat that presses upon his throat. The very words used to describe the Doctor at home are weighted words; he does not lie in his bed sipping chocolate; he sits up in his "chamber" in his "high" bed. He bears on his lap a silver tray with a silver chocolate pot. Next to his table are an Oriental gong and a bowl (not a box or a pack) of cigarettes. The room is dark and gloomy and holds a photo of his dead wife for whom, the narrative tells us, the Doctor pays to have Masses said, using her estate's money. He had once lived in France and could not forget it. As his servant walks in to tell him of Kino's request, the Doctor is "crumbling" a sweet goody in his fingers and having a second cup of chocolate. We also get to know something more directly about the Doctor through the analyses made of him by the four beggars at the church. They know of his ignorance, "his cruelty, his avarice, his appetites, his sins." They know about his abortions awkwardly performed, and his petty donations for alms. The portrait, in fact, is so blatant, that unless the reader remembers the trouble Steinbeck went to in order to emphasize the parable aspects of this novella, the lack of subtlety in character portrayals, he may very well see it as a parody-unconscious of course-of the personage under consideration.

CHAPTER II

Synopsis

The second chapter opens with a description of the beach on which the white and blue canoes of the natives are drawn up. They are preserved for generations by a specially handed down secret formula which preserves them from decay. Here, as in the first chapter, the novelist goes out of his way to detail the proliferation of animal and vegetable life. He mentions the presence of fiddler crabs, bubbling and sputtering (one remembers the little birds of the previous section who "chittered and flurried."), little lobsters, brown algae, green grass, sea horses, spotted botete (a poisonous fish), crabs, hungry dogs, hungry pigs. Steinbeck, in another one of those exploitations of nature **imagery** to further the readers' perception of some human attributes, discusses the quality of the morning at the beach. It is a hazy mirage, an unclear light which distorts or dispels some aspects of the scene. Thus sights are unreal; the eye cannot quite trust what it sees, and looks somewhat as in a dream. The people of the Gulf, says the narrative, were completely used to the blinding haze and the hot sun beating down upon the water, and would have been surprised that any place should be different. They trusted things "of the spirit," and things "of the imagination." The reader thereby receives an impression of the natives still further removed from, and at polar opposites of the kind of person and life represented by the Doctor. Kino and his wife come to the beach, to the canoe, that valuable commodity. They have the child Coyotito with them; she shields him from the sun with her shawl: he is quiet but the swelling on his shoulder has gone up to the neck, under the ear and into the puffed and feverish face. She makes a poultice from seaweed. Kino and his wife then go out into the sea, using their two double-bladed oars. Kino has two ropes, one tied to a stone and one to a basket. He drops in over the side, holding the rock in one hand and the basket in the other. Down under he searches for oysters. A song is in his mind, the Song of the Pearl that Might Be. Kino can remain undersea for two minutes with no strain, see a very large one, sees a ghostly gleam before it closes, so he works carefully, looking only for the largest oysters. He brings it up after he pries it out of its place. Once up he decides to open another, small, one first. But Juana, seeing his repressed excitement, asks him to open the big one; he does: it contains a pearl as large as a seagull's egg, "the greatest pearl in the world." She stares at it in his hand, the hand torn when he had smashed it against the Doctor's gate. She goes to the child, removes the poultice, and sees that the swelling is going out of the baby's shoulder. Kino holds the pearl tightly, puts back his head and howls. The men in the other canoes race toward Kino's canoe.

God and The Gods

Kino and Juana represent individuals caught in the relentless confrontations among the various realities of science, superstition, traditional lore and Western religion, in this case Roman Catholicism. Primitive societies are fast disappearing, and anthropologists are trying hard to investigate them and their social systems before they are irreversibly altered. The contending concepts which constitute the world in which the natives live are symbolized for the reader by a small phrase at the end of the description of the way an oyster secretes a pearl. The narrative emphasizes that finding a pearl is an accident, the product of luck or a fine gift by God or the gods. In this little aside commenting upon the monotheistic and pluralistic or animistic religions, the novelist imparts some of the changing realities impinging upon the natives. The tribal traditionalism which seems so secure to the two characters is in actuality in mortal danger of disruption and disintegration. We have seen, as a matter of fact, that when Coyotito is threatened by the scorpion in the first Chapter, his mother instinctively pronounces first an ancient magic spell under her breath, and then follows it with a Hail Mary, as if to show us the precedence of the older layer of religious belief. But there are no more mentions of Christian prayers. Rather, the narrative points out that Kino's people had sung of everything that had happened or been: songs to the sea, both in anger and pleasure, to the fish, to the light and to the dark, to the sun and moon.... And these songs, it should be pointed out, probably have their beginnings in some sort of sacred context. The mention of animism above should remind the reader that for a culture that worships the indwelling spirit of things, whether of animals, trees or water, chants of praise to such substances or living organisms partake of religious observances. So we see that the actuality of the life which Kino and Juana lead is eminently that of the older layer of their society, with surface grafts borrowed from the white invaders. Even the method used by Juana to attempt a cure of her son, the seaweed poultice, is described-in a sudden departure from the point of view of the narrative-as a remedy which is probably as good as anything the white Doctor could have prescribed, but lacked his authority, the authority of Science, not understood but feared in its mystery, and respected. Steinbeck usually tries to keep the point-of-view in the narrative pretty closely connected to the actual thoughts and perceptions of his native protagonists, but in the case above, the reader has the feeling that his feelings ran away with him, to the degree that the continuity is somewhat disrupted.

The Canoe

The reader has a strong sense that Kino could almost give a biography of the canoe, that for the native his boat has its own reality, almost an animal reality. It is this sense which makes it possible for Steinbeck to allow his character to own a valuable piece of property without thereby entering upon the category of possessors which the range of the novelist's fiction consistently damns. The relationship between Kino and his canoe comes in part from the fact that the boat had been handed down to him by his father, who in turn had gotten it from his father. In addition, another significant point is made in regard to the canoe. It is at once property "and source of food." It is "a bulwark against starvation." This is not pleasure boating, killing game for the fun of it, or expenditure of thousands of dollars on luxury sailing. Thus what a man needs to survive for himself and his family, the minimal economic necessity, confers upon ownership the grace of appropriateness and removes from possibility the ugly stain of avarice.

Kino

In this Chapter Kino is shown in action, working without pear at his learned craft. He works with "pride and youth and strength," the craftsman sure of his powers and confident of his skills. Like those of other "heroes" of Steinbeck novels, Kino's bodily grace and aptness at his chosen tasks combine with his sense of accomplishment at his specialty to present him as a somewhat special person. But unlike such heroes as Slim (*Of Mice and Men*), Billy Buck (*The Red Pony*), and Doc (*Tortilla Flat*), the young hero is in no position to be able to intelligently and maturely judge the workings of people and **episodes** as they pass on through his life. Their detached, somewhat passive and mature wisdom is denied to him, partly because of his youth, partly because of his insular social position, which has given him no experience with which to confront another culture. When Steinbeck dealt with the deprived in other novels, he did not underplay their hard lot, but did situate them within a culture which, manipulative as it might have been, and obstinately uninterested in their plight, was still theirs. The migrant laborers in *Grapes of Wrath* could not have been much worse off, but they were Americans and living in America, where everybody spoke one language, shared essentially similar monotheistic religions, and shared some sense of nationhood. When Kino goes to visit the Doctor, he gets only as far as the gate; the man who greets him there is another native, in the employ of the Doctor. To this man Kino speaks in the "old language." When the servant finally closes the gate on his fellow native, he does so quickly "out of shame." The necessity of living in such a bifurcated world is impressed upon the reader not only through the confrontations between different cultures, but also by the mere descriptions of Kino's daily life and environment, which must of necessity seem alien to almost every reader of this American book. The tense excitement at the discovery of the great pearl by Kino is to no small degree due to the fact that it is envisioned as some sort of magic talisman which will open doors, transmit messages through a kind of sudden Esperanto of economic power, alter the old exploitative relationship between one old culture and another. It is this tension which the young protagonist must allay by throwing back his head after the discovery, and screaming. His body was "rigid," we are told, almost as if it cannot bear the possibility inherent in the marvelous pearl, and must itself, in the unbearable moment, turn to stone.

CHAPTER III

Synopsis

Everyone in town knows the news almost immediately. The Doctor hears the news, and remembers his past in Paris. The beggars in front of the church hear the news. The pearl buyers hear the news. People with things to sell and "favors to ask" hear the news, which stirs up something "black and evil" in town. But Kino and Juana, unaware of these germinations, consider the world a friend to their joy. For Kino the music in the pearl joins with the Song of the Family. The house is full of neighbors. Juan Tomas, Kino's brother, asks him what he will do with the pearl. Kino sees in the glow of the pearl the possibility of marriage in a church, in full dress; they will have new clothes, a new harpoon, a rifle. That last mentioned really excites the neighbors, who would never have hoped to see one of theirs own such a valuable. Kino sees his son in the pearl, his son in a real school, which Kino had once seen through an open door; Coyotito will learn how to read, and "make numbers." After all the talk, Kino becomes suddenly afraid he has spoken too much. He had never talked so much at one time in his life. Everyone feels it is a historic time; Kino's life will be dated from this day on, and, for that matter, theirs too. The priest comes into the house; he tells Kino that he is named for a Father of the Church, who tamed the desert-it is in the books. Kino senses the slightest presence of the Song of the Enemy; he looks around to see which neighbor might have brought in the Song. The priest is shown the pearl, is told by Juana that she and Kino will now be married, and in the church. After the priest leaves, the Doctor enters, with an assistant, the servant who had opened the door. Hatred and fear fill Kino, as they had before. He curtly tells the Doctor the baby is nearly well. The Doctor assures Kino that nothing is sure; scorpion bites can be injurious after all signs point to recovery. The Doctor then examines the child, states that the poison has gone inward, gives the child a capsule of white powder, and tells the mother that the poison will attack in about an hour, at which time he will return. The baby soon is wracked by stomach spasms, vomits and writhes. The Doctor hurries in, examines the child, gives Coyotito three drops of ammonia mixed in water; the baby relaxes and sleeps. When can Kino pay? As soon as the pearl is sold. Ah! he has a pearl does he? Perhaps the Doctor can keep it for him, safely. The Doctor sees Kino's eye flit involuntarily toward the floor near the side post of the house. Alone, in the dark, his wife asks him whom he fears. He says, "Everyone." They go to sleep, but Kino is restless; he hears something outside, rises, strikes at it with his knife and misses, gets struck in turn. The assailant runs away, leaving Kino with a bloody head. Juana swabs his head. She asks him to get rid of the pearl; it will destroy them. He insists his son must go to school. Finally dawn comes and with it the promise of better things. He picks at the ground and sets his pearl up in the light. He smiles, and because they are one, his wife smiles too.

The Language

The conversational English used in *The Pearl* contrasts interestingly with the quality of language found in the dialogues of other Steinbeck novels. In many of his works, the novelist attempts to blend the realistic, or naturalistic, level with the symbolic. Sometimes the combination proves successful; at other times the reader is suddenly and forcibly removed from one kind of narrative action and asked to submit himself to a symbolic element which strains the credulity and tends to hamper the flow of the story. In *The Red Pony*, for instance (the interested reader may refer to the first half of this book), the disclosure is made that an old, dying paisano carries with him on his "last" voyage an antique Spanish sword, burnished and bright, and besides that nothing of any value. One thinks of *Don Quixote*, the famous Spanish picaresque novel, in which the "hero" is quite capable of such acts, but commits them in a fictional context which is a complex mixture of parody and sentiment. But here we are asked to take the old paisano's sword literally, and with total seriousness. Critics may debate the effectiveness of the device in this case. The essential reason for the sense of an abruptness in transition lies in the fact that *The Red Pony* is largely narrated with great attention to realistic detail. It is generally advisable that the symbolic incidents rise organically out of the realistic level of a narrative, rather than open up a new and alien line of story-telling. These considerations bear directly upon the language used by the characters in *The Pearl*. We know, according to the introductory paragraphs (commented upon previously) that we are not to look for a clearly naturalistic or realistic treatment of life in this story. Nevertheless the beginning of the story, as we have pointed out, teems with various forms of life appropriate to the environment, and creates a naturalistically convincing setting for the life activities of Kino, Juana and Coyotito. Whereas such a novel as *Of Mice and Men*, for instance, is essentially composed of dialogue within a dramatic and almost staged setting, *The Pearl* goes on for more than four pages at its start without a word of dialogue being spoken by anyone. Now *Of Mice and Men* is a book in which a distinct effort is being made to approximate in dialogue the "ungrammatical" and colloquial modes of speech representative of Americans in a particular place and time. But what was Steinbeck to do with dialogue in *The Pearl*? His speakers, after all, are not Americans; they speak in either the "old language" which Kino used in addressing the Doctor's servant, or, one takes it, in Spanish. And here we come to a crucial and critically vulnerable aspect of this novella, a problem involving the naturalistic and the symbolic ways of looking at the world. The novelist could have chosen to present his characters speaking colloquial American English; he chose not to. He seems to have chosen a linguistic path which eventuates in an old bastardization of two language directions. Some of the time the characters speak as if their original Spanish had been literally translated - not idiomatically. For instance: when the servant of the Doctor goes to talk to his master, he says to Kino, "A little moment; I go to inform myself," a sentence which reads as if it had been translated, poorly, from the original Spanish by the second-year high school student. At other times the characters speak in a vaguely lofty, rhetorically reaching prose reminiscent of possible Biblical antecedents. This second path is the one generally met in the novella, and it is a path by means of which the novelist tries somehow to create characters rather larger than life, elevated to quasi-mythic proportions, august in their speech. But whether the effort is successful remains uncertain. It would appear that where he can, Steinbeck discards dialogue in favor of descriptive prose, and so avoids the problem for that while. But the difficulty keeps cropping up. Although we know that the novella is intended as a parable, and we attempt to meet it more than half-way in good-will, responding to the author's sense of fairness and his obvious love of people and hatred of duplicity, we find it hard to accept such talk as this from Kino. "... my son will write and will know writing. And my son will make numbers, and these things will make us free because he will know - he will know and through him we will know." Even this passage may find some naturalistic justification, since it is spoken as Kino's face "shone with prophecy," and is thus a heightened moment of speech. But in many other cases he will say, for instance, "... the loss of the pearl was a punishment visited on those who tried to leave their station," or "what have I to fear but starvation?" or "Let us sleep a little. In the first light we will start," or such inconsistencies of speech patterns as that revealed in Kino's occasional use of the contractive "don't ... didn't" along with frequent usages of "did not ... do not." The merging of naturalistic and symbolic-or mythic-elements thus poses many problems.

The Doctor

This character is portrayed as increasingly hateful and amoral. He is dishonest not only toward others, but even in reference to his own memories. The news about Kino's pearl reaches the Doctor as he sits with a patient, to whom he explains that the man is a client of his, whose son is being treated for a scorpion sting. At that point his eyes roll up "in their fat hammocks" and he thinks of Paris, his room there and the "hard-faced" woman with whom he lived. He remembers the room as beautiful, the woman as lovely and kind: the narrative voice informs us that none of these recollections squares with the facts. When the Doctor makes his appearance at Kino's house, he earns the reader's hatred once again by his crude and sadistic recital of detailed injuries in possible store for the boy. Nothing will exercise the righteous imagination as piercingly as the commercial exploitation of parents based on their love for their children. The Doctor mentions the possibility of a withered leg, a blind eye, a crumpled back, "my friend." And the narrative twice more refers to the Doctor's eyes "in their little lymph-lined hammocks," and the eyes which "watered in their little hammocks." As the introductory comments notified us, it is indeed a portrait of black and white, with no saving graces inherent; he is a monster. In addition, we meet again "the fat fingers" which place the capsule in back of the baby's tongue; we see the Doctor, before his return to Kino's home, settled in his chair, nibbling "the little fallen pieces of sweet cake" and finishing his chocolate. He is in fact the incorporation of a number of medieval deadly sins, avarice, gluttony, lechery.

The Fish and The Mice

We saw in an earlier chapter that Steinbeck occasionally likes to intercalate passages descriptive of some aspect of the natural order, in order to suggest some analogies with the human order. The first instance had to do with Kino watching the ants fighting each other, and lording it over them like a detached deity. In Chapter III we find another one of these paragraphs. It is placed between the Doctor's two visits, the first when he placed the white powder in the baby's mouth, the second at which time he pronounced Coyotito saved. The paragraph describes a school of small fishes in the estuary which "glittered and broke water" in order to escape a clutch of larger fishes which drive after them to eat them; it also mentions the fact that the people in their brush houses could hear the swish of the little fish and the splashes of the big ones. In addition, the paragraph mentions the night mice creeping on the ground, and the night hawks pursuing them quietly. The moral applications are obvious.

BRIGHT NOTES STUDY GUIDE

Juan Tomas and Apolonia

Juan Thomas is Kino's brother, Apolonia his brother's wife. They initially appear in the first chapter, briefly, when with all the neighbors they pour into the house where Coyotito has just been bitten by the scorpion. We know of them only that Apolonia is "fat," that Juan Tomas is Kino's elder brother. They reappear later.

The Group-Animal

A brief mention can be made here of the particularly Steinbeckian nature of the paragraph which opens this third Chapter. The Introduction to this volume discusses Steinbeck's concept of the "group-animal"; it is the totality of organisms which go together to create one large superindividual organism capable of activity different in kind from that practiced by individual members of the group. Here in the first paragraph, Steinbeck gives another instance of this concept by comparing the town to a colonial animal, that is, an animal composed of various colonies of smaller animals. A town, we are told, has a nervous system, a head, shoulders, and feet; it is separate from other towns and has its own unique life; it incorporates its own emotional state. In it, by some almost mystical and secret process, news seems to travel faster than physical speed could account for. These considerations also suggest an interesting reaching back to an earlier time during which the now-commonplace words (head of a family, arm of the law, finger of justice …) still had a vivid, organic significance.

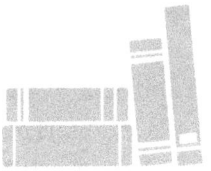

THE PEARL

TEXTUAL ANALYSIS

CHAPTERS IV–VI

CHAPTER IV

Synopsis

The citizens of the town supposed that the pearl buyers were competing business men. Once this was so, but the passage of time had shown that too high a price would sometimes be paid for a pearl. Now there was only one central pearl buyer and the various "individual buyers" in town were merely his hirelings. On this day, Kino and his wife go to sell the great pearl. They dress carefully, Juana putting on her marriage skirt, tying her hair with red ribbons, Coyotito dressed in the clothes saved for his baptism. As they step out of the house the neighbors, as well as Juan Tomas and his wife, join them in their march toward town. The brother warns him not to be cheated. The procession is solemn. In their offices the pearl buyers grow alert and tense. They remove any pearls from their desks tops, for a comparison would not favor them. Kino enters one of the offices, shows the dealer his pearl.

BRIGHT NOTES STUDY GUIDE

The dealer examines it ... and tells Kino he is sorry. The pearl is too large, like fool's gold it is, no market for it, just a curiosity. It is large and clumsy. Perhaps it is worth 1000 pesos as a curio for a museum collection. Kino cries out that it is worth 50,000. The appraiser, somewhat abashed at the grumble from the listening crowd, suggests that other dealers be brought in to judge. None of the other dealers of course credit the pearl with any value. Kino snatches the pearl away from the pearl buyers, and says he will go to the capital. That upsets the buyers; the man at the desk says he will give fifteen hundred. But Kino strides away, furious.

Some of the townspeople praised Kino for his courage; some condemned him for his foolhardiness: for a penniless man 1500 pesos is a good deal of money. In his house Kino sits brooding; he is afraid, never having been out of his village; he is terrified of the capital, more than a thousand miles away. But he has lost his old world and must trudge on to another one. His dream is compelling. Juan Tomas talks to his brother, agrees that now the fat is in the fire. Kino must go to the capital, but he reminds Kino that there are no friends there. Kino, after his brother's departure, is depressed and lethargic; he does not move, does not ask for supper. The night is coming closer; he senses something out there: he suddenly walks out, knife drawn. Juana seizes a stone from the fireplace to help out her husband. But the struggle is soon over, her husband half-conscious, a deep cut from ear to chin, his clothes torn. She wipes off the blood with her skirt. He does not know who it was. She asks him to throw the pearl back into the sea; it is evil. He insists upon his way; they must go to the capital. They sleep.

Kino

This Chapter furnishes more details about his behavior. When Kino gets ready to go into town to discuss the sale of his pearl with the appraisers, he puts on his large straw hat. This is not unusual, but the narrative goes into some detail about the exact way he places it on his head. He does not put it on the back or side of his head, like a "rash, unmarried, irresponsible" man; nor does he wear it flat, like a sober and too old citizen; he tilts it forward a little, to show his assertiveness and virility. As he walks toward the town, in the company of his brother and his neighbors, we are told that his eyes, as well as those of Juan Tomas, squint a little. They squint like those of the grandfathers, and the great-grandfathers before them. They have squinted like that for four hundred years of being subjugated by the invading strangers. It was and is their only defense against the guns and the authority and the rule of the aliens - the slitting of the eyes, the constriction of the lips, the withdrawals. Within that fortress of privacy they can remain inviolable, and whole. It avails them mostly, of course, when they are the butt, when they are assaulted; it avails them less when they are the ones who go forth to make demands, when they actively enter that other world and act to some degree within the accepted modes of it. And this is the root cause of Kino's great fear of the capital city. But within the context of his retinue, and his confidence in the pearl's worth, the young man is able to spontaneously summon forth his sense of the dramatic: when the first dealer asks to see the pearl, Kino does not immediately produce it; he brings out a leather bag, and slowly removes a soft and dirty piece of deerskin from it, then lets the pearl roll into the pearl tray. After the rejection by the dealer, however, Kino's buoyancy and optimism turn to the fear and hate which are the product of a growing awareness of the malignity of fate. Typically Steinbeck personifies these feelings of Kino's; they are not merely the creeping of fate; they are also "circling of wolves ... hover of vultures." He hears the evil music. But he cannot retreat from his intended journey to the capital.

The Pearl Buyer

Here we see another example of the general rule that the good have names, the evil do not. We never find out the name of the appraiser; he is always "the dealer." And like the Doctor, he is malign, though his face is "fatherly and benign." His eyes have a warm glow of friendliness. He is described as a shaker of hands, a greeter, a jokester who would suddenly remember the death of one's relative and grieve for the loss. He shaved close; his beard has blue roots; his hands are clear, his fingernails polished. Steinbeck makes these simple details bear the burden of corruption. In the Steinbeckian lexicon of moral worth, sophistication always threatens honesty; the clever, as we also learn in *Of Mice and Men*, are seldom the trustworthy. And polished nails won't do.... As he waits he hums a tune under his breath and practices trick handlings of a coin with his right hand. He rolls the coin back and forth over his knuckles, making it appear and disappear. The dexterity is high, but the dealer does not even watch his own skill; he performs mechanically, a symbolic reminder to the reader that for this man expertise in a craft is merely an automatic, mechanical trait, unconnected with the whole man-a significant symbolism when we recall that for Steinbeck the hero is always the man who has mastered a certain craft, and derives a great amount of pride and spiritual strength from the knowledge. The coin is equally and more obviously symbolic as it comes and goes more and more quickly just as the figure of Kino comes into the doorway. Money, property, economic advantage.... Now Kino is bearding the lion in his den. The dealer hides the right hand behind the desk as he interviews the young man, but does not stop his practicing, until he sees the pearl, at which point the coin slips into the dealer's lap. But this is the only sign of the appraiser's amazement, and of course not perceptible to Kino, on the other side of the desk.

The Sermon

During a conversation with his brother, Kino has occasion to refer to a sermon expounded by the priest year after year. In the sermon the priest tells his congregation that the old ones had acted against religion when they tried to sell their pearls in a different way. The pearl divers once tried to get a higher price for their finds by appointing one man as messenger to bring all the pearls to the capital, where he could get a better price than that offered by the wily merchants of the town. Unfortunately the messenger was never heard from again and the pearls were lost. The old ones tried it a second time, with no greater success. That doomed the plan. The priest went on to explain that everyone occupies a certain place in the world and should not try to go beyond that place, otherwise he is in danger of assaults from Hell. So here we see that the forces tending to hold down Kino in his search for justice, in his passionate desire for other horizons, are indeed powerful. The story about the sermon is interesting from another point of view as well. We have seen previously that Steinbeck's sympathies tend toward the more primitive, the less sophisticated, the rural rather than the urban, the simple and traditional rather than the movemented and upwardly mobile. But the world which elicits such sympathies is also one in which the appearance of stability often rests to a significant degree upon pressures capable of keeping every citizen "in his place."

Juan Tomas

Kino's brother acquires in this Chapter a mantle of worldly-wisdom, tempered with mature understanding, which is denied to his younger brother, who is learning things very much the hard way. Juan is to Kino as experience to innocence, as speculative detachment to passion. It is hard to know what to do, he tells his brother; no one knows the real value of pearls, but all know they are underpaid. Kino's complaint is justified, but there will be isolation and suspicion in the capital: the ground is new, the way unknown. He is afraid for his brother. When Kino says that his friends will protect him, his brother more wisely answers that they will do so only as long as they are in no danger or discomfort from such protection. They wish each other goodbye, "Go with God," but the words have a "strange chill" in them.

CHAPTER V

Synopsis

Kino, in bed, opens his eyes in the dark. He feels some movement in the house. His wife gets up silently, moves the fireplace stone and glides out. Enraged, he gets up; he follows her to the water's edge; as she is ready to throw the pearl into the sea he grabs her arm, and strikes her in the face with his fist. She falls. He kicks her in the side. He turns back, filled with a sick disgust, to the house, where he is assaulted by a shadowy figure, which he stabs, but himself is knocked down as the pearl rolls behind a stone. Juana, in the meantime, drags herself up and after washing her face goes back to find her husband. She sees the pearl behind the rock, glimmering, and picks it up, then glimpses her husband and another figure with a fluid dripping from his throat, dead. She drags the dead man into the brush, goes to Kino and sponges his face with her skirt. He moans about the stolen pearl; she tells him she has found it, and that the man is dead. They must leave before daylight. Though it was, as he says, in self-defense, nobody will believe it, she assures him. He stumbles to his canoe, find a large hole in it. Suddenly he sees flames leap up. Juana runs toward him, Coyotito in her arms. The house is destroyed; as she looked they burned it after ransacking it. He asks who did it. She does not know. He steals into his brother's house with his wife and child. From inside they hear the mourning cries of Apolonia, who with the rest of the village considers them dead. She rushes to her house to get her best heads hawl for mourning and Kino tells her quietly they are not hurt. He sends her to get her husband. Kino tells him about the murder. Juan Tomas says the pearl has a devil in it. Perhaps there is still time to sell it and buy some peace. Kino counters with the story of the punctured canoe. His home, his boat, and the dead one in the brush: every escape is cut off. Kino asks Juan Tomas to hide him, just for one day; they will leave at night. The brother agrees to hide them. Juan Tomas orders his wife to keep absolutely quiet about Kino's presence. All day they sit in the darkness of the house, able to hear the talk about them from neighbor's houses; through the brush walls they can see the villagers raking the ashes to find their remains. Juan Tomas himself goes among the neighbors to allay suspicion. The wind rises that day, making the sea unsafe for navigation. Juan Tomas tells some neighbors Kino must be dead now if he took to the sea. Toward evening the brothers talk; Juan Tomas advises his younger brother to avoid the shore: the city men will be on the lookout. The wind will help hide the fugitives' tracks. When the time comes to go, the brothers embrace with a special embrace. Juan Tomas asks his brother for the last time whether he will not give up the pearl. No; the pearl has become Kino's soul; if he gives it up he gives up his soul.

Juana

We were previously informed that Kino valued his wife for her endurance under stress. In this chapter, we are actual witnesses to that endurance. When Juana is struck on the face and kicked in the side by her husband, she neither resists him nor protests. There is, we are told, "no anger in her." For the very traits which make him assault her are inextricably woven in with that self which makes him the man she loves. For her, Kino's recent statement, made in rebuttal to her suggestion that he get rid of the pearl - "I am a man," he had said - means that he is "half insane and half god." She knew what it meant: that he would contend with a mountain and be broken for his pains. But he could do no other; and she can do no other than accept him in his wholeness. That she will follow him anywhere never is questioned. Steinbeck, in this section of the chapter, attributes certain qualities not merely to Juana, but to "woman." They are consistent with some of his views toward what we have called traditionalist society; in any case, they are not attributes which would be accepted as universally female in our culture. They include "... the reason, the caution, the sense of preservation...." virtues which the modern psychologically-oriented world would tend to grant not so much to a particular sex as to a particular temperament, regardless of sex. A large number of women characters in Steinbeck's fiction demonstrate the novelist's idiosyncratic portrayal of them. While, as we have seen, it is true that many male characters are often not treated in depth, the configuration of female characters is even more generalized. Curley's wife, the only female character in *Of Mice and Men*, is never even given a name; neither is Jody's mother in *The Red Pony*: she is Mrs. Tiflin, the fulfiller of certain traditionally assigned female tasks; she fills a category.

Kino

As the novella gathers momentum, we see Kino's subjection to an increasing intensity of the experience of evil. And it seems that his cup of that experience is running over. He is beset not by one, but by both of the two main categories of evil: the wickedness implicit in the immoral activities directed towards him and his family in non-physical terms, and the acts of vengeful, splenetic destruction wreaked upon him. It is hard to say whether the reader can establish any clear hierarchy in the first category. Is the avaricious and malign Doctor more or less evil than the cynical and defrauding dealer and his associates? While the first plays with the life of a child, the second plays with the economic life of the family. The vicious assaults made upon Kino physically: one man against another in the dark; the destruction of his canoe; the burning of his home. Interestingly the Song of the Enemy, or the Song of Evil, seems to invade Kino's consciousness more readily in the context of vices more relevant to the first category. The Song connotes the lurking dangers of the hidden and mysterious operations of malice, operations fraught with vaguer, less definable - and therefore more frightening - viciousness than relatively direct and personally physical assaults. It is easier to deal with the meter reader who comes to our homes every two months than with the complex, abstract and potentially difficult Gas and Electric Company. By the time Kino has passed through this Hell of trials, the pearl has indeed become his soul, and the tragic direction of the tale is clear from this point. The passionate intensity of Kino's reactions to injustice is a radical and dangerous straying from the concept of life as a series of necessary accommodations. Juana and Juan Tomas, both of whom love Kino and go so far as to risk their lives for him, are the only ones with the requisite familial intimacy and moral power to induce him to abandon his interest in the terrible pearl. When they fail, he is doomed; the evil has been absorbed; like the pearl it is part of him, and will disintegrate him. Kino knows of no way to deal with the evil when he meets it outside of himself: the institutional repressions are too powerful to contend with. On the other hand, he refuses to surrender to the reigning order of injustice, rejects the possibility of a viable, if bitter, peace with it: thus he must incorporate it, try to bridge the enormous and mystery-laden gap between innocence and experience. Unfortunately the entire situation has had too great a magnitude to enable him to learn and to absorb what he has learned-and then to act self-protectively. His expectations of what the pearl might do for himself and his family demonstrate the insufficiency of his understanding of his cultural status. Thus he gains knowledge useful to his entire people at the cost of his own soul.

Apolonia

She never blooms as a completely realized character. Her one active participation in the novella comes in this chapter and is a traditionally sanctified and prescribed action of mourning. She goes back to her home to put on her best head shawl not so much because of a personal sense of grief (although this sense, as far as we know, is incontestable) but prompted to this action by the formal customs of her people. She, as the nearest woman relative, is responsible for the official lamentations.

Juan Tomas

Her husband, on the other hand, grows greatly in stature in this chapter. Experience has tempered him, but fate has graciously allowed him to benefit from his experience; in addition he is not cursed with the fiery rejection of the middle way characteristic of his brother. And it is precisely because of his finely developed sense of survival and self-protection that his courage in hiding Kino and Kino's family constitutes an act of such courage. For Juan Tomas is going against the grain of what life has taught him, and his resolution of the conflict about hiding his brother places him in the role of hero almost more than his own brother, who is driven and seems to have no choice. The hero is usually the man who has a choice and makes the difficult one. He reminds the reader of the ranchhand Billy Buck, in *The Red Pony*, a member of the line of Steinbeck heroes, who also conquered an experimental and temperamental aversion when he allowed a brood mare to die in order to salvage the infant foal which had been promised to his employer's son. Juan Tomas, in the interview with his brother, first takes the tack of caution and advises his brother to get rid of the pearl-which is what he himself would have done, no doubt. When this advice is rejected, he courageously allows Kino to stay, although he disapproves of his brother's obduracy. Then, having given shelter, he demonstrates wisdom in the advice to Kino and Juana to stay away from the coastline.

CHAPTER VI

Synopsis

The wind is strong as the fated couple leaves, avoiding the center of town. Kino, though frightened, also experiences a feeling of exhilaration. As they go they see no one. They walk all night; at dawn Kino finds a place off the road to sleep in, and erases their footsteps with a leaved branch. They eat some of Apolonia's corncakes. After his wife has slept, Kino sleeps a little but stirs suddenly, listening. In the distance he sees three figures, one on horseback. The trackers....! Although Kino and Juana had walked carefully in ruts made by wagon wheels, they might have gone onto ordinary flat surfaced sand on occasion, and these trackers were known for their expertness. If the trackers find the swept place Kino is ready to jump the horseman, take the rifle and kill the others. It is the only chance. But they go by after stopping to examine the spot. He knows, however, that they will be back. He is in a panic of flight. He suggests that they surrender. Juana asks if he thinks the trackers will let them leave after stripping him of the pearl. They then decide to go into the mountains. There he tells his wife to hide; he will go on, lead them into the mountains and she will go on north to a town. He will meet her there if possible. She refuses. His resolution returns. They keep going, moving upward in large zigzags. They find a spring and drink. Way down in the valley he sees the pinpoints which are the trackers. He helps Juana and Coyotito up into a shallow cave, warns her to try to curb the baby's crying. Kino sneaks down to where the three men have made camp. He moves with agonizing slowness. Then he is twenty feet away from them and starts to loosen the knife his brother had given him; but dawn comes up just then; he retires behind a bush. At that moment Coyotito cries; the men wonder if it might be a coyote. The child cries again. Just to make sure the rifleman lifts his weapon and shoots. And precisely as the bullet leaves the rifle Kino leaps, grasping the rifle as he loosens his knife. He fatally stabs the rifleman, and goes through the second man's head as if it were a melon; the third man slips down. Kino kills him with the rifle. A terrible cry, the cry of the lamentation for death, sounds now. The baby has been murdered. They return to the town, Juana carrying the little limp bundle, removed "as Heaven," both of them "removed from human experience." They walk through the town as if alone, though surrounded by silent people edging away to let them pass. They go to the sea. His hand shakes a little and he hands the pearl over to her. But she, still holding the dead child, says, "No. You." He throws it into the sea with all his might. The music of the pearl disappears.

The Ants Again

The reader will recall the appearance in the beginning of this novella of two kinds of ants in a struggle viewed by Kino from a perspective of divine detachment. Ants appear again in this last chapter, but with a different symbolic significance. Where they represented the young protagonist's sense of optimistic satisfaction in the first chapter, they now play a darker role. Soon after the start of their journey, harbored temporarily in the covert by the side of the road, Juana sleeps. While she does Kino sits on the ground and stares at the earth. A column of ants is moving near his foot. He deliberately places his foot in their path, but the column climbs over his instep and, undeterred, continues onward. He does not move his foot, just sits and watches them move over it. The symbolic significance, here as in the first chapter, is obvious.

Descriptive Precision

This final chapter contains some very precise nature description, demonstrating Steinbeck's familiarity with the wild. The description of the little pool in the mountains, for example, is not a quick superficial or merely symbolic apparition. The animals which come there to drink are not generalized, but enumerated. The wild sheep and the deer come, and the pumas and the raccoons, and the mice. The birds also, having spent their days in the brushland, come at night to the pool. And beside the little stream, in the presence of enough soil for roots, grow wild grape, palms, maidenhair fern, hibiscus, tall pampas grass with "feathery rods raised above the spike leaves." In the pool gather frogs, water-skaters, waterworms. Steinbeck also mentions that this is the place where the big cats take their prey, leaving feathers around. The water makes this area a place of life, but a place of death too. Near the end of this chapter, we find a descriptive passage which unites both the objective view of the natural world with the subjective life throbbing inside Kino. He is in the process of stealing toward his three enemies at night.

The narrative makes very specific the kinds of dangers implicit in the production of the wrong sounds: a rolling pebble, "a sigh, a little slip of flesh on rock." Any sound he made would have to fit in with the noises of the small tree frogs near the stream that "twittered like birds," with the "high metallic ringing of the cicadas." The Music of the Enemy and the Song of the Family clash in the young man's head, and the Song of the Family is "as fierce and sharp and feline" as the snarl of a female puma. The cicada sounds seemed to absorb the melody of that Song and the frogs apparently called out little phrases of the Song.

The Two Songs

The Song of the Family and the Song of Evil reach the height of their symbolic significance in this last chapter. Under the influence of the exhilarated lift in his spirits which follows his experience of fear of the unknown path, Kino is able to let the "music of the pearl" play in him; and accompanying it is the "quiet melody" of the family. But directly afterward, when he is talking to his wife, he looks into the pearl in order to see his good future reflected in it, as he had when he first joyously celebrated his good luck; but his vision has become a nightmare. He says he will buy a rifle when he sells the pearl; he looks into it and sees only "a huddled dark body on the ground" with glistening liquid dropping from its throat; he looks into it to see his future marriage in a great church and sees only his wife with the marks of his beating upon her face, crawling home in darkness; he looks into it to see his son at school, learning to read, and sees only Coyotito's face, distorted and fevered by the act of the Doctor. He then puts the pearl back into his pocket and never looks at it again until he throws it away.

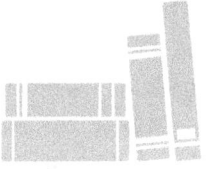

THE PEARL

CHARACTER ANALYSES

Kino

A young man, married with one son, Coyotito, a mere infant. The dreadful series of incidents which haunt his and his family's life when he finds a magnificently large and opalescent pearl taxes him beyond his capacity to integrate his experience to the point of self-protective wisdom. He is represented in the beginning of the novella as a rather average member of his village, living in exactly the same kind of brush house as his neighbors, earning an almost microscopically small living by pearl-diving like them and owning the same kind of canoe as they do. But he is most probably different from most of his neighbors in the quality of his reactions to the finding of the pearl and to the iniquities of the world. The difference would not have been apparent in his daily life with his co-citizens; it was a compound of unverbalized hopes and dreams which would probably never have risen into consciousness had it not been for the extraordinary discovery. He had a highly passionate nature, unwilling to temporize or follow a thoughtful path of reason. But his headstrong nature does not provoke the reader's impatience, since the combination of circumstances (including his child's near-death and the

Doctor's cynical machinations) serves to largely justify the extremity of his reactions. He is a master at his craft of pearl-diving, and those excellences of physical grace and youthful reflexes (in which he delights in an almost childlike fashion in the beginning) also come into exciting and stealthily admirable use when he is fighting for his family's life like a well-trained killer animal.

Juana

Kino's wife. A woman in whom the traditional female virtues of patience, obedience, dependability and loyalty are paramount. She is described as being able to bear the great pains of childbearing without a word, as being equal in agility and skill to a man when canoeing. She is seen in action as stalwartly daring to pursue a course of action which she knows hateful to her husband. Such a choice is only possible because she is willing to risk his everlasting hatred by performing an act which she considers will save the entire family's existence. When in his fury he smashes her face with his fist, she has no complaint to make: he is what he is, and she loves him through it all, basically convinced of his undying love for her as well. She is a devoted mother whose care and sympathy for her infant boy are without flaws. Her carriage is graceful; her relationship to others in the village, as far as can be intuited, seems good. In spite of her apparent humility, she can be very assertive when she considers that such an attitude is warranted by the needs of her husband or child; it is she who suggests going to the Doctor, a visit never before made by any of her people, who probably rely on a combination of traditionally herbal remedies and superstition. So in her way she is, in emergency situations, as atypical an example of her people as her husband is.

Juan Tomas

Kino's older brother. Kino looks to him for wisdom and advice. He is a man whom experience has tempered but not corrupted or made hard. He has no illusions about his neighbors; he has no quarrel with them, but knows that they might not be dependable if a situation in which their help is required also promises them a certain discomfort. At the risk of his own and his family's welfare, he allows his brother to remain hidden in his home for an entire day, thus exposing himself to the same institutional villainies that have so grievously afflicted Kino. He has learned better than his brother how to bear insult and injury and the contempt of the conqueror by withdrawing into the private self. He is not capable of the romantic ardors of his beloved brother, but does not condemn him or them.

Apolonia

Juan Tomas's wife. We know little about her. She is fat, conventional and plays almost no part in the action, except that she acts as the official mourner of Kino's family when they are supposed to have been killed in the fire which decimated their home.

The Doctor

A creature so void of human sympathy, so full of cynicism, so egotistically dishonest, so avaricious, so contemptibly hypocritical that he seems almost a **parody** of a man, rather than a fully fleshed human being. His motives are transparently visible to the entire town; he has no skill at duplicity. He is a glutton, is portrayed as guzzling porcelain cup after porcelain cup of hot chocolate with dainty goodies. He is authoritative with his servant and contemptuous of the natives, or anybody else, for that matter, who is in no position to advance his materialistic desires. He dreams endlessly about his distorted fantasy recollections of his past days in Paris and lives in a house characterized by its dark, heavy, tasteless and pretentious environment. He is perfectly able and willing to administer harmful medications to a little child if such activity has a chance of adding eventually to his worldly goods.

The Dealer

An apparently paternal, jovial and sympathetic appraiser and buyer of pearls, whose affable mannerisms serve as a screen to mask real intentions: to buy for a price so absurdly low as to make even the unsophisticated villagers knowledgeably angry. He is represented as a man skilled in certain mechanics of stage magician's crafts, but one completely uninterested in the craft, only involved in the mechanics. This involvement has its analogy in his attitude toward the potential sellers who come before him; he is utterly uninterested in anything about them except the degree to which he can demonstrate to his employer his ability to fleece them.

The Priest

He only appears once, briefly, on the occasion of Kino's return home after the discovery of the great pearl. The scene shows him as the purveyor of pious platitudes, eager to encourage some contribution to his church. He is also mentioned, by Kino in conversation with Juan Tomas, as the author of a sermon delivered every year: in it he emphasizes to his native parishioners that they are all put on earth to fill a certain place, the keeping of which is an act of piety. Any wandering from one's station, as determined by birth, is an irreligious act. The villagers at one time, long past, attempted to get higher prices for the pearls which they dove for at great peril. This attempt, which met with ill-luck on two occasions, had to be abandoned, and the villagers were forced back onto a complete dependence on the corrupt pearl dealers in town. The priest seized this occasion to brand the villagers' attempts as a breach of faith and of divinely appointed place.

Coyotito

An infant, the son of Kino and Juana.

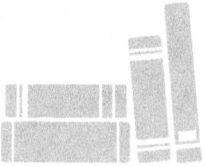

THE RED PONY AND THE PEARL

CRITICAL COMMENTARY

The amount of criticism devoted to *The Red Pony* and *The Pearl* is, as could reasonably be expected, not anywhere as plentiful as the analyses concerning Steinbeck's longer works. Some critics, however, have made various comments about both novellas, and we will list below the views of seven of them.

PETER LISCA'S VIEWS

Lisca has written probably the most extensive essay on *The Pearl*. He praises Steinbeck for his success in creating a sense of the folklore environment in this book. Although the action is simple, it suggests underlying planes of meaning. And these suggestive areas involve not only the pearl itself, but the characters and settings as well. Lisca points out that Kino's assailants come at night, perceived only as vague shadows; the young man calls them "things"; his wife calls them "the dark ones"; the man on horseback pursuing the fleeing youth and his family is a vague "dark man," and all three pursuers are referred to as "the dark trackers." This critic emphasizes his conviction that *The Pearl* contains some of Steinbeck's best prose, distant yet intimate, "like a medieval tapestry." He stresses the successful application of the technique of objective narration, a procedure that enables the novelist to ward off any possibility of sentimentality in the telling of the story. He has also written about *The Red Pony*, stating that these four **episodes** have an extremely successful style, combining a confrontation of violence with "a rhythm and a tone more akin to the idyllic and pastoral than to the naturalistic." He calls the reader's attention to Steinbeck's construction of a "middle distance" in the work, a perspective by means of which we can sympathize with the characters but remain delightfully apart from the action. It is this distance, Lisca says, which makes it possible for the novelist to avoid the pitfalls of sentimentalism which so often afflict stories having to do with the lives of children.

RAY B. WEST'S EVALUATION

In a book on the American short story, West occasionally calls Steinbeck to account for the novelist's overly folksy manner. But he singles out *The Red Pony* as a good story, not among the best in the century, but an earnest attempt at focusing upon man's natural instincts; he also praises Steinbeck for demonstrating in *The Red Pony* an attempt to underline values more lasting than those suggested by most of his contemporaries. West judges Steinbeck to be a good, minor writer.

FREDERIC I. CARPENTER'S OPINION

Carpenter considers *The Red Pony* "brilliant." In his opinion, the four parts announce the novelist's artistic maturity, and his achievement of "complete realism." Carpenter underlines the sense of reality in this work, but calls attention to the fact that the red pony is also the symbol of "the old American dream." Jody becomes the man on horseback, an extension of a dream. But the red pony is too highly sensitized to survive the difficulties of a life on a ranch; he is a show horse. The birth of the little foal in the third section of the book is an event which Carpenter sees as announcing the need that the younger generation must be able to fill: a need for its own experience of the land, not a dependence upon the traditions of the past, beautiful as those may well be.

JOSEPH WARREN BEACH'S PRAISE

Beach finds in *The Red Pony* examples of human types and relationships as fine and as subtle as any in the writings of the great Russian storyteller Anton Chekhov. He praises Steinbeck's capacity for communicating the boy's world in a natural setting. He heartily underlines the excellence of the depiction of Jody's relationship with his "stern but just and loving" father. And he believes that the finest presentation of all may be found in the figure of Billy Buck the ranchhand.

JOHN S. KENNEDY'S DISAPPROVAL

In an essay on Steinbeck's work, Kennedy quotes some heavy critical guns in his purposeful attempt to demonstrate Steinbeck's essential and fatal weaknesses. He quotes Edmund Wilson's often-repeated comment that Steinbeck has an "animalizing tendency," an attitude which presents human beings in animal terms. He also quotes Alfred Kazin, who wrote that Steinbeck approaches the modern social struggle "as a tragicomedy of animal instincts." Kennedy, a representative of Catholic critical points of view, says that he quotes these non-Catholic critics in order to demonstrate that his own view, which is comparable to theirs, does not emanate simply from a provincial moralistic attitude. He refers to Steinbeck's habit of making parallels between man and animal behavior as "blatant and hideous" in one particular case, and cites another example of what he dislikes in this habit from *The Pearl*. He is unhappy with the way in which the novelist portrays the role of the priest, and inferentially the Church, in that novella. He considers Steinbeck to be saying that the Church is "obscurantist," that it is guilty of "the unscrupulous milking of the poor." But Steinbeck, Kennedy states, never really comes to grips with the basic Christian religion, and thus never takes into account what it has to say about human nature and destiny. He refers to Steinbeck as a sentimentalist, a harsh criticism. Nor does he exclude *The Red Pony* from his displeasure. He cites an instance from *The Red Pony* in which dogs hunting mice are compared with soldiers hunting Native Americans, and finds the parallel irritating. Man is an animal, but a rational one. And Kennedy accuses Steinbeck of lowering the essential moral nature of man.

A FRENCH VIEW

Claude-Edmonde Magny finds that for Steinbeck evil is always devoid of ambiguity; he is a man, she finds, who believes human beings are good by nature. These convictions give him confident strengths to create books characterized by an almost "pre-Edenic innocence," which leave the reader refreshed. She cites a comment by Jody's Grandfather, in *The Red Pony*: what the old man wanted to communicate was not just the old stories of the Westward trek, but the way in which the entire convoy was transformed into "one big crawling beast." It is this transformation that she finds the novelist to be successful in achieving. She finds most admirable this sense of a kind of magical transmutation which Steinbeck is more adept in writing about than some French novelists like Jules Romains, whose avowed aim is precisely what the American achieves. She believes Steinbeck is a writer who finds the grandeur in collectivism, rather than its ugly sides. But she reproaches him, conversely, with creating characters whose simplicity makes them not very human. They are little individualized, their emotions remain obscure, they have no clear consciousness of themselves. She also states that Steinbeck's universe sadly lacks a sense of evil. She maintains that the reason for the success of *The Red Pony* lies in the fact that the real heroes of that novella are the animals, not the people.

WOODBURN O. ROSS'S JUDGMENT

Ross, in a brief comment on *The Pearl*, considers it "not important," but reflective of the novelist's love of the primitive life. He finds that Steinbeck's essential trouble lies in the fact that he is "a man of two worlds." He believes in the scientific method of objective description; but he also reflects powerful and irrational attitudes. And he is therefore an unhappy mixture of brutality and tenderness, rationality and irrationality, a combination incapable of ultimate synthesis.

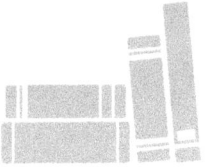

THE RED PONY AND THE PEARL

ESSAY QUESTIONS AND ANSWERS

Question: Who is the hero of *The Pearl*?

Answer: If the answer to this question is based upon the frequency of appearance and the bearer of the greatest proportion of the plot line, then obviously Kino is the main **protagonist**, the hero. But a reasonable answer must entail a concept of the hero consonant with Steinbeck's usual "hero-figure," and if this yardstick is applied, there are some very important ways in which Kino does not fill the role. Steinbeck's usual hero combines a few attributes. He has a detached awareness of the impersonal and sometimes cruel processes of the natural world, he is a good craftsman, he is compassionate, and he tends to be thin. Kino is lean; he is a good diver. But his youth and hot-blooded immediacies of reaction to injustice do not permit much detached awareness and preclude a continuous possibility for compassion. It is Juan Tomas, his brother, who embodies these virtues much more clearly. But Juan Tomas appears so briefly that he cannot easily be categorized as the main figure. Thus a certain ambiguity pervades any attempt at answering this question, an ambiguity which does not necessarily weaken the story.

Question: How does Steinbeck represent woman in these two novellas?

Answer: In both cases women are presented more in terms of a generalized and idealized series of functional operations than as complex human entities. Mrs. Tiflin, Jody's mother in *The Red Pony*, is never called by her first name. Her time is spent cooking, cleaning, telling Jody what to do, tenderly empathizing with the boy. The reader has no idea about her interior, subjective life. In only one case does the intensity of her emotions propel her to a transgression of the habitual patterned roles in the ranchhouse. This occurs when she defends her father, whose tendency to repeatedly tell the same old stories drives her husband mad. Juana's behavior in *The Pearl* is a similar pattern-breaking transgression: she too is generally obedient to her husband's will, but trespasses on his preserves when she judges the situation has become a familial threat. It is appropriate that Juana's effectiveness rests primarily upon her traditionally "feminine" qualities and not upon any show of force, over-assertiveness or originality of personality. Such effectiveness, the traditional "power behind the throne," is also what characterizes Mrs. Tiflin and other female **protagonists** in Steinbeck's work.

Question: In what way does animal **imagery** serve to illuminate human behavior in Steinbeck's fiction?

Answer: The novelist will often insert one or more paragraphs at particularly significant junctures in his stories. These paragraphs serve to point up the unity underlying all forms of life, a concept which for Steinbeck is of the highest importance. His position is that these intercalations are not placed for the purpose of demeaning the moral position of man, but are used in order to demonstrate in a dramatically effective manner the poetic appropriateness of **metaphors** based on the animal world.

Question: A number of important American literary critics have not seen fit to discuss Steinbeck's work in any great detail; why is this so?

Answer: This century has been the period of subtle and complex psychological analysis par excellence. A number of influential critics, for whom the unconscious proliferations of dreams, fantasy, buried wishes, forbidden thoughts, and murky motivations constitute perhaps the most important aspect of a contemporary understanding of man, find Steinbeck sadly lacking in such concerns. He is usually satisfied to sketch his characters rather shallowly and makes no serious attempt to represent with any directness the torrent of unconscious conflict and ambiguity typical of the human mind and its daily activities. A number of critics have found fault with him for his "animalization" of man, for his descent into representing morons, happy-go-lucky bums, shiftless hedonists and characterless women. They find in him very little understanding of the maze of human ambivalences. They point out that his sense of evil is rudimentary and permits of no subtle analysis of differentiation of degrees, such as life readily offers to all men.

Question: Who was Ed Ricketts, and why was he very important in shaping the thought of Steinbeck?

Answer: Ricketts was a marine biologist, a close friend of the novelist's. Discussions and trips for specimen-collecting were shared by both men, and some of the biological observations which resulted from their investigations played a role in forming some of the novelist's concepts. The reader will find in *The Pearl*, for instance, several passages in which the novelist envisages a town as a functioning organism, with its own circuits, its proper limbs and organs and vessels. This way of looking at the town has its basis in Steinbeck's discovery that certain forms of marine invertebrates, when clustered together in a very large colony, will act as if they were one large animal, with its own sensory perceptions, and with the ability to provide adequately for itself. These speculations may be found in *Sea of Cortez*, a journal of an expedition kept by Steinbeck and Ricketts. Steinbeck was also intrigued by the idea of a group-memory, the possibility that in some not-quite-explainable and quasi-mystical manner a group could somehow experience a recall of past events in a way peculiar to itself. From Ricketts Steinbeck absorbed the pattern of scientific objectivity, which of course was no stranger to his personality. And it is this pattern, which, joined to his passionate feelings about the land and its animals, served to produce a creative personality at once objective and highly reflective of emotional involvements-a personality which became the butt of many critical tirades complaining about the novelist's essential inconsistency of vision.

Question: Is Kino's ultimate defeat, in *The Pearl*, a glorious and "romantic" one, or is it essentially the result of a foolish pride?

Answer: The word "romantic" offers one of the keys to an intelligible answer to this question. Writers in the nineteenth century, members of what is known as the Romantic persuasion, often glorified individuals characterized by a passionate nature rebelling against established institutions, which they decried as sham-ridden, filthy with class distinctions, and oppressive. The individual who could be categorized as a revolutionary became The Hero. The celebration of individual freedom was emphasized. In such a context, it can be seen that Kino could easily be described as a hero, and his defeat as the necessary but glorious fall of a superior man fighting a gallant fight against impossible institutional odds. In American literature Captain Ahab, the skipper of the whaleboat which went seeking for the great whale Moby Dick, is often analyzed as a type of romantic revolutionary who hurls his challenge in the teeth of Fate. On the other hand, Kino's revolutionary decision to go to the capital in order to sell the great pearl himself could be seen as the foolhardy act of a narcissistic youth whose concern with the satisfying of his own vengeance and the appeasing of his own needs jeopardized his whole family's future. And again, one could maintain that Kino, his family and their existence are every bit as institutionalized in their own particular culture as is the middle class society Steinbeck is forever critical of. The answer depends upon the context.

Question: What aspect of man's social behavior does Steinbeck seem to most deplore?

Answer: Steinbeck apparently finds much of the root of social evil in the act of possession. Owning something of value-unless it is clearly associated with survival like Kino's canoe, or with tradition and craft like Jody's house, or earned by great sacrifice, again like Jody's foal-brings about a corruption of the soul, because it enshrines a materialistic concern rather than a cultivation of direct compassionate concern for one's fellows. Avarice, which has to do with the accumulation of wealth, pushes men like the Doctor in *The Pearl* to brutal and inhuman behavior. The pearl dealers are reduced to mechanical copies of men. They have no feelings, no compassion for the poor and needy who come before them. They are concerned only with paying the lowest price. It is no accident that the important figures in both *The Red Pony* and *The Pearl* have, we take it, no bank accounts. Gitano, the old mysterious paisano, owns almost nothing at the end of his life's wanderings; Billy Buck is a simple ranchhand, not a middle-class employer; Kino is excrutiatingly poor; Juan Tomas has almost nothing.

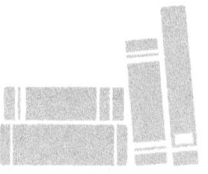

BIBLIOGRAPHY

EDITIONS OF THE RED PONY

Steinbeck, John. *The Red Pony*. New York: Covici-Friede, 1937. Deluxe edition only, 699 copies, numbered and signed by the author. Contains "The Gift," "The Great Mountains," and "The Promise," all previously published. Later printed in *The Long Valley*.

Steinbeck, John. *The Long Valley*. New York: Viking, 1938. Includes for the first time the fourth part of *The Red Pony*: "The Leader of the People."

Steinbeck, John. *The Red Pony*. New York: Viking, 1945. Illustrated. Contains all four sections of the novella.

Steinbeck, John. *The Short Novels of John Steinbeck*. New York: Viking, 1953.

EDITIONS OF THE PEARL

Steinbeck, John. "The Pearl of the World." *Woman's Home Companion*, #72, December 1945, pp. 17ff.

Steinbeck, John. *The Pearl*. New York: Viking, 1947.

Steinbeck, John. *The Short Novels of John Steinbeck*. New York: Viking, 1953.

BOOK-LENGTH STUDIES OF STEINBECK'S WORKS

French, W. *John Steinbeck*. New York: Twayne, 1961 (a good general summation).

Lisca, Peter. *The Wide World of John Steinbeck*. New Jersey: Rutgers University Press, 1958. (The first detailed study of most of Steinbeck's output. Perhaps still the best.)

Moore, Harry T. *The Novels of John Steinbeck*. Chicago: Normandie House, 1939. (The first full-length study by any critic. Interesting as far as it goes. Quite fair in accenting strengths and weaknesses.)

Tedlock, E. W., Jr. and C. V. Wicker. *Steinbeck and his Critics*. Albuquerque: University of New Mexico Press, 1957. (Absolutely invaluable collection of critical essays, on both general **themes** and individual works. Several short statements of interest by Steinbeck himself. Very useful introductory survey of criticism.)

Watt, F. W. *John Steinbeck*. New York: Grove, 1962.

SELECTED GENERAL BIBLIOGRAPHY

Beach, Joseph Warren. *American Fiction, 1920-1940*. New York: Russel and Russel, 1960.

Fairley, Barker. "John Steinbeck and the Coming Literature" *The Sewanee Review*, April-June 1942.

Frohock, W. M. *The Novel of Violence in America*. Dallas: Southern Methodist University Press, 1957.

Geismar, Maxwell. *Writers in Crisis: The American Novel 1925-1940*. Boston, Houghton Mifflin, 1961.

Hoffman, Frederick J. *The Modern Novel in America: 1909-1950*. Chicago, Regnery, 1951.

Howard, Leon. *Literature and the American Tradition*. Garden City: Doubleday, 1960.

Kazin, Alfred. *On Native Grounds*. New York: Harcourt Brace, 1942.

Spiller, Thorp and Canby Johnson. *Literary History of the United States: Bibliography Supplement*. (ed. Richard Ludwig) New York: Macmillan, 1959.

SUGGESTIONS FOR RESEARCH PAPER TOPICS

1. Compare Kino and Billy Buck

2. Steinbeck's attitude toward women, as revealed in the two novellas

3. The significance of Steinbeck's home area in *The Red Pony*

4. The nature of Steinbeck's objectivity

5. Depth psychology in *The Pearl*

6. Ritual in *The Pearl*

7. The balance between naturalism and lyricism in *The Red Pony*

8. Steinbeck's descriptive powers

9. The use of poetic techniques in *The Pearl*

10. The influence of Ed Ricketts on Steinbeck

11. *The Pearl* as parable

12. *The Red Pony*: a look at American tradition

13. The similarities between Gitano and Grandfather in *The Red Pony*

14. Compare Mrs. Tiflin and Juana

15. Steinbeck's use of verbs in *The Pearl*

16. Compare the quality of dialogue in *The Red Pony* and *The Pearl*

17. The relationship between the symbolic and the realistic in *The Pearl*

18. The place of these two novellas in Steinbeck's work

19. The role of animals in *The Pearl* and *The Red Pony*

20. Billy Buck as a culture hero

EXPLORE THE ENTIRE LIBRARY OF BRIGHT NOTES STUDY GUIDES

From Shakespeare to Sinclair Lewis and from Plato to Pearl S. Buck, The Bright Notes Study Guide library spans hundreds of volumes, providing clear and comprehensive insights into the world's greatest literature. Discover more, faster with the Bright Notes Study Guide to the classics you're reading today.

See the entire library of available
Bright Notes guides at **BrightNotes.com**

Available in print and digital wherever books are sold

IP INFLUENCE PUBLISHERS

www.ingramcontent.com/pod-product-compliance
Lightning Source LLC
LaVergne TN
LVHW011730060526
838200LV00051B/3102